Jossey-Bass Teacher

Jossey-Bass Teacher provides educators with practical knowledge and tools to create a positive and lifelong impact on student learning. We offer classroom-tested and research-based teaching resources for a variety of grade levels and subject areas. Whether you are an aspiring, new, or veteran teacher, we want to help you make every teaching day your best.

From ready-to-use classroom activities to the latest teaching framework, our value-packed books provide insightful, practical, and comprehensive materials on the topics that matter most to K–12 teachers. We hope to become your trusted source for the best ideas from the most experienced and respected experts in the field.

PREVIOUS BOOKS BY MICHAEL GURIAN

PARENTING

Nurture the Nature

The Wonder of Children (previously published as *The Soul of the Child*)

The Wonder of Girls

The Wonder of Boys

A Fine Young Man

The Good Son

What Stories Does My Son Need? (with Terry Trueman)

PSYCHOLOGY

What Could He Be Thinking?

Love's Journey

Mothers, Sons and Lovers

The Prince and the King

EDUCATION

The Minds of Boys: Saving Our Sons from Falling Behind in School and Life (with Kathy Stevens)

Boys and Girls Learn Differently!: A Guide for Teachers and Parents (with Patricia Henley and Terry Trueman)

The Boys and Girls Learn Differently Action Guide for Teachers (with Arlette C. Ballew)

BUSINESS/CORPORATE

The Leading Partners Workbook (with Katherine Coles and Kathy Stevens)

FOR YOUNG ADULTS

Understanding Guys

From Boys to Men

FICTION AND POETRY

The Miracle

An American Mystic

The Odyssey of Telemachus

Emptying

As the Swans Gather

PREVIOUS BOOKS BY KATHY STEVENS

The Minds of Boys: Saving Our Sons from Falling Behind in School and Life (with Michael Gurian)

Leading Partners (with Michael Gurian and Katharine Coles)

Strategies for Teaching Boys and Girls— Secondary Level

A WORKBOOK FOR EDUCATORS

By Michael Gurian, Kathy Stevens, and Kelley King

JOSSEY-BASS
A Wiley Imprint
www.josseybass.com

Published by Jossey-Bass
A Wiley Imprint
989 Market Street, San Francisco, CA 94103–1741—www.josseybass.com

Jossey-Bass books and products are available through most bookstores. To contact Jossey-Bass directly call our Customer Care Department within the U.S. at 800–956–7739, outside the U.S. at 317–572–3986, or fax 317–572–4002.

Jossey-Bass also publishes its books in a variety of electronic formats. Some content that appears in print may not be available in electronic books.

ISBN: 978-07879-9731-1

Printed in the United States of America

FIRST EDITION

PB Printing   10 9 8 7 6 5 4 3

About This Book

*S*TRATEGIES *for Teaching Boys & Girls: A Workbook for Secondary Level Educators* is an invaluable resource for teachers working with students from sixth through twelfth grade. It weaves together brain science, adolescent development, and classroom strategies in a way that is both easily understandable and immediately applicable. This is the kind of book that teachers want—one that combines the right balance of "just enough" theory to help teachers become knowledgeable and a "whole bunch" of practice so that they can jump right in with the strategies on Monday.

We've organized this book around several important strategy domains so that you can go right to the sections you need. We do suggest that you start with Chapter One to lay a foundation about the brain. After that, feel free to skip around to the parts you most need as a teacher. You'll find chapters on movement, visual teaching strategies, social interaction, offering choice, art and music integration, making learning relevant, and more. Each of these chapters provides you with a fascinating look at how the brain works and illuminates why these strategies are so important for all learners. Central to each chapter is an exploration of the differences between the male and female brain and the connection of these hardwired differences to gender-specific teaching strategies. We think you'll appreciate the comments from students about their own learning, as well as the anecdotes from teachers about what works in the classroom.

The highlight of this book is the extensive list of classroom activity and strategy ideas that span all content areas. We wanted to create a book for teachers that can be read and re-read many times and that will be a source of creativity and inspiration for years to come. We hope that our ideas may infuse a new level of excitement, curiosity, and student learning in your classroom.

The Authors

Michael Gurian is a social philosopher, family therapist, corporate consultant, and the *New York Times* bestselling author of twenty books published in twenty-one languages. The Gurian Institute, which he co-founded, conducts research internationally, launches pilot programs, and trains professionals.

As a social philosopher, Michael has pioneered efforts to bring neurobiology and brain research into schools, homes, workplaces, and public policy. A number of his groundbreaking books in child development, including *The Wonder of Boys, Boys and Girls Learn Differently!, The Wonder of Girls,* and *What Could He Be Thinking?*, as well as *The Minds of Boys* (coauthored with Kathy Stevens), have sparked national debate. His newest work, *Nurture the Nature* (2007), provides a revolutionary new framework, based in neurobiology, by which to understand and care for children all the way from birth to adulthood.

A former university instructor, Michael has worked as a consultant to families, therapists, schools, school districts, community agencies, and other organizations. He keynotes regularly at conferences and has lectured at such leading institutions as Harvard University, Johns Hopkins University, Stanford University, and UCLA. His training videos are used by Big Brother and Big Sister agencies throughout North America.

Michael's work has been featured in various media, including *The New York Times*, the *Washington Post, USA Today, Newsweek, Time, Educational Leadership, Parenting, Good Housekeeping, Redbook,* and on the *Today Show, Good Morning America*, CNN, PBS and National Public Radio.

Kathy Stevens, executive director of the Gurian Institute, is an international presenter and coauthor of *The Minds of Boys*. Her work has been featured in national publications including *Newsweek, Reader's Digest, Educational Leadership, Education Week, National School Board Journal,* and *Library Journal*.

Kathy has over twenty-five years of experience working in the nonprofit sector, focusing on children, youth, families, and women's issues. Her professional experience includes teaching music in Pre-K–8, designing and administering programs in early childhood care and education, domestic violence, juvenile corrections, adult community corrections, teen pregnancy prevention, cultural competency, and women's issues. Much of her early work was done in economically disadvantaged minority communities.

In addition to her work with the Gurian Institute, Kathy has designed and delivered training for the Federal Bureau of Prisons, Virginia Department of Corrections, Girl Scouts, U.S. Navy Ombudsman Program, Disproportionate Minority Confinement Task Force and a variety of nonprofit organizations. As a diversity trainer, she was honored to participate in the Children's Defense Fund's Institute for Cultural Competency at the former Alex Haley Farm in Tennessee.

Kathy lives in Colorado Springs with her husband. She has two sons and seven grandchildren.

Kelley King, director of the Gurian Institute's education division, has been a classroom teacher, special education teacher, teacher of the gifted, and a school administrator for twenty years.

While a school principal, Kelley initiated and led her school through an improvement process targeted at closing the gender gap, including the analysis of the data, professional dialogue and training, and the identification and implementation of effective strategies. Through action research, she has been able to demonstrate the effectiveness of *The Minds of Boys* and *Boys and Girls Learn Differently!* theory to enhance the achievement of all students.

Through her work with the Gurian Institute, Kelley presents at schools and conferences across the United States. Her work has been featured on The Today Show and in national publications including *Newsweek* and *Educational Leadership.*

Kelley and her husband, Chris, live in Superior, CO with their two children.

About the Gurian Institute

If you would like to help your school and community better understand how gender affects learning and living, please contact the Gurian Institute. Through our four divisions—Education, Family, Human Services, and Corporate—we provide training and services to schools, school districts, institutions of higher education, parent groups, businesses, youth-serving organizations, juvenile and adult corrections, medical and mental health professionals, religious organizations, and others serving boys and girls, and men and women.

We also provide keynotes and breakouts at conferences worldwide. There are Gurian Institute trainers throughout the United States, and in Canada, Australia, China and France.

We are committed to helping school districts, corporations and agencies become self-sufficient through internal training-of-trainer models. These are ongoing and serve populations over the long term.

A highlight of our training year is our annual Summer Training Institute, in Colorado Springs. Professionals join together for four days of training and networking. Some individuals become certified on the fifth day.

The Institute also provides books, workbooks, training videos for educators and parents, newsletters for parents and teachers, online courses and live chats, as well as other products.

For more information on services, products, and our philosophy, please visit www.gurianinstitute.com.

GURIAN
INSTITUTE

Acknowledgments

TEACHING is both a craft and an art. Each new teacher arrives in the classroom with a toolbox filled with ideas, strategies, passions, and hopes that will be transformed into opportunities for children, boys and girls, to learn how to read, add, subtract, think, ponder, and dream. With every passing school year teachers add new tools to their toolbox—they learn from professional development opportunities, from each other, from mentors, and they learn from the children.

The Gurian Institute has been invited into classrooms around the country, meeting wonderful educators who have honored us by allowing us to help them expand their toolbox. They have been the motivation and inspiration for this book. Dedicated administrators and teachers are working every day to understand how boys and girls learn differently, and by so doing help every student reach as high as she or he can. This book is richer as a result of teachers sharing their successes and students adding their voices. We are grateful to each and every one of them. We especially must acknowledge:

- Our Gurian Institute certified trainers, whose expertise and dedication carries them to hundreds of schools every year, sharing their knowledge and experience with their colleagues, practicing what they preach, improving the odds for each boy and girl who enters a classroom. Many of our trainers are educators just like you—principals, classroom teachers, curriculum specialists, school counselors—working in schools rich in diversity, challenge, and success.

- The outstanding educators in the Boulder Valley School District, especially Ellen, an exceptional mentor and role-model, and the magnificent teachers and staff of Douglass Elementary School.

- All the schools, teachers, administrators, and students who shared their wisdom and feelings with us—they make the book more real.

- The professionals who took time in their already over-booked lives to review the manuscript and offer invaluable feedback.

- The editorial staff at Jossey-Bass is simply the best in the business! The wisdom and support of Lesley Iura, Julia Parmer, Margie McAneny, Natalie Lin, Kate Gagnon, Pam Berkman, Dimi Berkner, and, as always, Alan Rinzler have combined to make it truly a better book than it would have been without their help.

Dedication

Michael: For Gail, Gabrielle, and Davita, and all the teachers.

———————

Kathy: To all the teachers who dedicate themselves daily to offer each girl and boy a chance to develop to her or his fullest potential. I am in awe!

———————

Kelley: I could not have participated in writing this book without the patience, understanding and support of my family. My husband, Chris, coached me to take it one step at a time as I pondered the magnitude of writing a book on top of being a full-time school principal. My children, Connor and Roxanne, were always so understanding when I sequestered myself in the study for long periods of time. They have been my greatest teachers about gender differences—as evidenced by my son's exasperated inquiry one night, "Why do you have to write a book? That just means that people like me have to read it."

Contents

About This Book   v

The Authors   vii

About the Gurian Institute   ix

Acknowledgments   xi

1   What Could They Be Thinking? The Science of Boy-Girl
    Learning Differences   1

2   Maximizing the Brain-Body Connection:
    Moving Through the Curriculum   17

3   Creating a New Playbook: Using More Visual-Spatial
    Strategies in Your Classroom   39

4   Building Learning Teams of Boys and Girls:
    Promoting Positive Social Development   59

5   Letting Them Lead: The Power of Choice on the
    Developing Adolescent Brain   69

6   When Am I Ever Going to Use This Again? Finding
    Ways to Make Learning Real   87

7   Reading Between the Lines: Figuring Out
    What Adolescents Will Read   109

8   Modeling the Adult World: The Crucial Role
    of the Mentor   127

9   After the Final Bell Rings: The Lives of Teenagers
    Outside School   141

Epilogue   157

Sources   159

Index   165

What Could They Be Thinking?

The Science of Boy-Girl Learning Differences

1

Instead of thinking about a teenage mind as an empty house that still needs furnishings, educators and parents would do better to understand it as the rough framing of a house that still needs wiring, plumbing, flooring, and windows. Avoid treating teenagers like adults; they're not.
—Eric Jensen

OVER the past couple of decades, exciting research into the living brains of males and females has shown us not only that boys and girls are different at the organic level but also that how they learn includes many differences, from the day they are born. In just the past few years, cutting-edge research has begun to help us better understand the learning styles of both male and female adolescents. We are better able than ever before to answer such questions as, What goes on in a male and female brain when puberty begins flooding the system with hormones? What happens to boys and girls when their bodies begin the transformation from child to young adult? What does it all mean for teachers?

Watching students pour into the halls when the passing bell rings in any high school, it's easy to forget that we're seeing children. Many are physically mature. Some of the boys are really tall, their voices deep. Some wear a shadow of a beard by noon. Some of the girls are shapely and dressed like women. They wear makeup and designer clothing. Often students are paired up, boy and girl, heading for their next class and making plans for after school and the weekend. They seem awfully sure of themselves.

But we are seeing children—children whose brains are still moving toward a maturity they won't reach for a number of years; children whose pubescent systems egg them on to take chances, seek novelty, ignore warnings, respond to impulses they don't fully understand. They are children who need strong, caring adult mentors and role models to help them navigate until their internal directional systems are ready to take over and lead them safely into the future. They need teachers to prepare them for life.

In the early days of the Gurian Institute's work with educators, we would ask the question "How many of you took a course on how boys and girls learn differently during your teacher training in college?" Even in audiences of several hundred educators, no hands would go up. When we ask that same question today, a few hands may go up. When questioned further, those who raise their hands generally report that they covered the topic of gender and learning briefly in an education class.

At the same time, when teachers attend our seminars and trainings, they often ask, "Why isn't this being taught in college? Why aren't schools of education teaching male-female brain difference? It affects every grade level." Fortunately, many schools are beginning to catch up to the newest brain research in learning, development, and gender. This workbook is part of that effort.

The Gurian Institute has spent twenty years developing materials and working in schools, training teachers in the practical strategies we have developed from what we have come to understand about how the male and female brains learn best. In this book, we are sharing what we know. You'll meet many middle school and high school teachers who will also share strategies they have learned and developed, and your teacher's toolbox will be increased manifold.

This chapter will give you an overview of the latest information available on how boys and girls learn differently and how that difference can and should change the way you implement your curriculum. We hope to help you ensure that every adolescent you teach, male and female, will have the chance to succeed to his or her maximum potential. Many of you will read this information and think "YES! This validates intuitions I've had for a long time." We hope it will confirm that you have been on the right path as you work with your students. We hope that for many of you, this information will open the door to exciting new experiences as you implement what you learn.

You may ask, How can I effect change in middle or high school when my students have experienced years of institutional schooling that may have inadvertently had a negative impact on them? Shouldn't this science and research change the way we educate our boys and girls from the very beginning? The answer is yes, and we work with preschool and elementary programs to help them lay a foundation that you can build on when the students reach your classroom. In the meantime, there is still much you can do; remember that the adolescent years are ones of great possibility and promise. We hope that the information in this book, and the resources beyond this book that we offer, will help you make a difference for every student you teach from today on.

From the Beginning, Boys and Girls Learn Differently!

Where does gender in the brain begin? Soon after conception, boys and girls are on diverging developmental paths. If a child receives an X chromosome from each parent, a female plan goes into action. If a child receives one X chromosome and one Y chromosome, a different plan is activated, and a male system is designed. These plans result not only in different bodies but also in different brains.

Beginning at around six weeks, a male fetus triggers the mother's ovaries to provide testosterone to his fetal system. As a result, his genitals drop and begin producing the testosterone he needs. From that point until somewhere between five and six months of development, testosterone becomes the "chief engineer" of the developing male's body and brain, giving him the capacity for a higher muscle mass than a female, different iron and calcium ratios, and different brain "formatting." Developing female fetuses receive testosterone during the developmental period between six weeks and six months in utero, but not as much. They receive more estrogen-type hormones. This helps format their brains to be female. By six months in utero, boys and girls have been formatted with different brains.

This early developmental groundwork is critical for the male and female brain, as it plants the seeds that will grow and flourish when puberty again floods the brain with sex hormones. Testosterone will surge through the male system more than once during childhood and in great amounts during puberty. Female hormones—more than thirty of them—will affect girls significantly during puberty and through the child-bearing years.

Are these differences all that matter? Of course not. There are many similarities between girls and boys in utero and after they are born. There are also many differences among girls and among boys that indicate how powerfully individual personalities affect ultimate development. Furthermore, the way a child is nurtured can affect how he manifests his maleness and she her femaleness. By the time these boys and girls saunter into your middle and high school classrooms, they share many characteristics—and they are at the same time very different. During adolescence, their male and female biology and chemistry will at times trump all other influences, making both their lives and yours really interesting.

Caveats aside, gender is a big deal—especially in learning. Understanding differences in how girls and boys learn gives us a head start in meeting that challenge of instructing and guiding young minds.

What *Are* the Differences?

Ongoing research is still discovering new areas of difference between male and female brains, but many differences have already been identified that have implications for how boys and girls learn. We'll present some of these to you now, and please remember that we are generalizing based on the best relevant research available today. There will be exceptions to everything we say, as every child is an individual and brain differences range both between boys and girls and among boys and girls. Remember also that difference means only that—one is not *better* than the other. Both are equally capable of learning and succeeding; they will just do so in ways that we must understand if we are to create an educational environment that meets the needs of both.

Structural Differences

Using *magnetic resonance imaging (MRI), positron emission tomography (PET),* and *single photon emission computed tomography (SPECT)* technologies, scientists can look at the living brain and watch it work. These advanced technologies let researchers watch actual blood flow in the brain, see where the brain is working, and, by looking at male and female brains in this way, see that they are working in different areas when completing the same tasks.

Over the past couple of decades, technology has helped researchers focus on some specific areas of structural difference between male and female brains. The following sections describe some of the differences and their potential impact on your classroom.

Cerebral Cortex—The cerebral cortex contains about ten thousand miles of neural connections in each square inch! From an evolutionary standpoint, the cerebral cortex is the "newest" part of our brain and significant in making humans different from all other animals. If you could spread the cerebral cortex out flat, it would be about the size of a newspaper opened up. In order to "fit" over our brain, the cerebral cortex folds into place. This area, only as thick as about three of your hairs, is where the serious intellectual functions of the brain take place. Thinking, speaking, and recalling—all things that need to happen in a classroom—are controlled in the cerebral cortex. This area also facilitates memory functions, voluntary motor behaviors, impulsivity, decision making, and planning—again, important for learning. The female brain tends to have more connections between neurons in the cerebral cortex, which also tends to mature earlier in the female brain.

And this means—the increased number and speed of the neural connections may help girls process and respond to classroom information

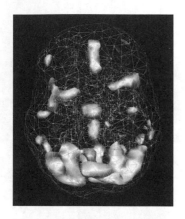

Scans of the Female Brain (top) and Male Brain (bottom) at rest. The areas you see that look like bubbles are areas of activity.

SPECT scans used by permission of Dr. Daniel Amen

faster than boys and help them make transitions faster, multitask, and access needed verbal resources (reading, writing, complex speech) better than the average boy as they engage in learning. Earlier maturity may result in girls' being less apt to engage in high-risk behavior, less likely to respond impulsively, and, in general, more likely to "think before they act." It might also explain why girls tend to gather and complete their college application forms earlier than boys!

Cerebellum—The cerebellum, larger in the male brain, was once believed to be mainly involved in the coordination of our muscles, making us graceful dancers and good athletes. But research has shown that it's also involved in coordination of our thinking, our "mental muscles." Adolescents might be described as going through a period of mental clumsiness (along with their obvious periods of physical clumsiness). The cerebellum seems to have the ability to smooth out the complicated social life of adolescents and help them navigate their world smoothly and gracefully instead of constantly tripping over themselves. Physical activity is believed to influence development of the cerebellum.

> *And this means*—for healthy development of the teen brain, including the cerebellum, activity is important. Today's students are less active overall—they are sedentary while watching TV, playing video games, talking on their cell phones—and not doing as much "playing." There is less recess and fewer hours of structured physical education classes, and fewer students walk to and from school. Bringing more movement into your curriculum will help both boys and girls, whose brains, including the cerebellum, are changing a lot during this period of life.

An example: while working with a school, grades 7–12, near Minneapolis, we spent a day observing classes, including watching the students do a marching demonstration for Grandparents Day. The teacher in charge of the ROTC program shared his frustration that the middle school and freshman boys especially had a really hard time learning to march in formation. "They just can't seem to get their feet going the right ways!" He was blaming himself for not providing the right instruction to help them "get it." After gaining a better understanding of adolescent brain development, he realized that many of the boys in the middle school and lower high school grades were simply suffering from adolescent clumsiness—he could see that it was a developmental stage. He was doing his best, and the boys were doing their best, but their bodies and brains were just not quite in synch with each other yet. The teacher's increased patience helped the students be less stressed about their mistakes, which decreased as they moved through each grade and developmental stage.

Corpus Callosum—The corpus callosum is a dense bundle of nerves that connects the two hemispheres of the brain; research indicates that this area increases in size during adolescence. In females, this bundle of nerves tends to be denser and larger than in males, resulting in increased "cross-talk" between the left and right hemispheres. The anterior commisure, a tiny additional connection between the hemispheres attached to the end of the corpus callosum, is also larger in females.

> *And this means*—girls are generally better at multitasking than boys, including watching and listening and taking notes at the same time. This gender difference may also help explain why girls tend to tune into their own and others' feelings and move emotional content more quickly into thought and verbal processes. Girls can tell you how they feel as they are feeling, whereas boys often need time to process before they can begin to explain their feelings. Combined with the hormonal changes during adolescence, the increased connections between thinking and feeling may account for the hypersensitivity and tendency to be dramatic that girls exhibit during adolescence.

Brain Stem—This is the most primitive part of our brain. Our "fight or flight" responses come from the brain stem, and when we're in crisis, this area of our brain takes over, telling the body how to respond. With a greater amount of spinal fluid connecting their brain and body, and increased levels of testosterone during this developmental stage, adolescent boys often respond physically and very quickly to stressors—hitting more and responding in other nonverbal, physical ways.

> *And this means*—boys' brains tend to be poised for fight or flight and for a physical response when they feel threatened or emotionally charged. Add to the equation the seven to ten significant daily spikes of testosterone that boys experience, and you may see volatility that can become a problem for the boys and their classrooms. Boys in your class may slam a book, kick a chair, use an expletive, or engage in some other kind of physical display when they feel threatened. And remember, a threat at this age can include being challenged by an adult in front of a boy's peer group. Status in the group is very important during adolescence, so adults need to evaluate carefully when, where, and how to confront these kids.

Limbic System and the Prefrontal Cortex—The limbic system, a collection of structures located deep in the brain's interior, is closely associated with emotional responses. The fear response to your car spinning out of control on the ice or the joy of getting an acceptance letter to your first-choice college can bring the same kind of biological emotional response. Emotional responses in the limbic system try to move to the prefrontal cortex, the part of the cerebral cortex that lies just behind the forehead and acts as a sort of mental traffic cop. In adolescents, this movement is often slowed by hormones and a lack of developed brain connections between the limbic system and the prefrontal cortex. An adult, for instance, who observes a group of people looking in his or her direction and laughing might feel an emotional response in the limbic system, but probably won't respond in any way because the prefrontal cortex would say, "It's okay." An adolescent might make the assumption that the people were laughing at him or her and become upset, angry, or defensive. Adolescents just might not be as good as we think they are at interpreting facial expressions and nonverbal signals, in part because the prefrontal cortex is not yet lending the limbic system a hand.

Within the limbic system are several structures that play a key role, both on their own and as they connect to the prefrontal cortex, in how boys and girls learn and perform differently. Parts of the limbic system that process emotion and sensory memory are, in general, more active in girls than in boys, resulting in increased emotional memory for females, and better reading of emotional cues.

- *Hippocampus.* This is a key player in converting information from working memory into long-term or permanent memory. The hippocampus is crucial for learning and for retention. It tends to be larger in females, and the speed of neural transmissions is faster than in males, contributing to generally increased emotional memory storage for the female brain.

- *Amygdala.* This is a small, almond-shaped structure connected to one end of the hippocampus; it plays a very important role in the processing of emotions, especially negative emotions, such as fear and anger. The amygdala tends to be larger in males, possibly explaining the male tendency to be more aggressive. Some researchers believe that the close proximity of the amygdala to the hippocampus suggests that emotional content may be "tagged" onto many long-term memories. Consequently, recalling a memory can recall an emotion as well. Note: reducing the activity level of the amygdala brings us closer to a state of "happiness" by calming down the negative emotional response system. Performing nonemotional tasks (for example, folding laundry, doing the dishes, doing some exercises) can help this calming-down process. The calmer an adult can remain when dealing with an agitated adolescent, the better the chances of the event's not escalating. Someone has to be the most mature member of the group!

And this means—boys often display increased aggressive or impulsive responses when they feel angry or threatened—they tend to be sent to the principal a lot more than girls! Immediately after they have been involved in an altercation, they find it much more difficult to explain how they were feeling, needing more time to process the event and understand the feelings. Girls tend to attach more emotional and sensory detail to events and remember them longer. They can hold grudges a long time. They often need mentoring in order to see what really is important about a situation and what is hyperreactivity. Defusing emotional situations will help both boys and girls calm down and get back on track. Note: playing calming music can help change the brain state in the classroom.

Blood Flow in the Brain—Blood flow is up to 20 percent greater in the female brain. In conjunction with the increased neural connectivity between hemispheres, this adds more potential for information to move quickly between areas of the brain.

And this means—again, there is generally increased speed of communication between hemispheres and between different areas of the female brain, allowing for quicker processing, especially of verbal information. Note: sometimes this increased speed of communications can be problematic for girls—they may not always "think before they speak," tending to process *as* they are speaking. Slowing that process down is tough for adolescent girls, but slowing down could help minimize conflict in peer and adult relationships.

The male brain will tend to take a little longer to process verbal and emotional information. This can affect behavior, and it can also affect reading and writing. Girls generally read more, write more, include more sensory and emotive details in their writing—getting better grades! More graphic analysis (visual and pictorial) can help boys write better papers, as we'll see in this book.

Processing Differences

Studying images of the working brain, researchers find that the brains of males and females differ not only in terms of structure but also in terms of how they process information. Knowing about these differences can become quite important as you develop strategies to implement your curriculum in ways that will allow both boys and girls to perform at their best.

Language Processing Areas—Whereas males' language processing areas tend to be centralized in the left hemisphere, females have multiple language processing areas in both hemispheres. As a result, females have more access to verbal resources than males and generally develop language earlier than males.

And this means—girls tend to have significantly more access to verbal resources when they start school, and throughout life, than boys. On average, females use twice the number of words that males do (this includes writing and reading). It is easier for them to learn to read and write in kindergarten and first grade. Because literacy is the foundation of learning, this early difference often results in gender gaps that show up early in elementary school and persist throughout middle and high school.

Spatial Processing Areas—Testosterone, the primary architect of the male brain, is believed to create more and denser neural connections in the right hemisphere of the male brain, resulting in males' having increased resources for spatial reasoning—mental manipulation of objects, gross motor skills, spatial-mathematical reasoning, and abstract spatial reasoning. With less testosterone at work during fetal development, females tend to have less right hemisphere area devoted to spatial resources. (A crucial note: although boys in general test higher than girls in spatial manipulation tests, there is less of a gender gap in mathematical calculation. Girls are not worse at math, as has been the stereotype in the past. They just tend to be so good at literacy skills that they don't get enough opportunity to practice using their spatial capacities; then, when girls need those skills to be sharp, the skills are not as ready to be engaged.)

And this means—boys tend to need more space in which to function while they are learning, need to move in physical space more during learning, and are generally more interested in spatial manipulation tasks. As we'll see in this book, it is crucial to employ strategies that help girls gain parity in science and technology classes. Boys are significantly more interested in computer games than girls; they enjoy moving through the virtual space of the games, most of which offer lots of chances to win and advance to higher levels. This sense of reward can set boys up to play too many video games, at the expense of good learning. Girls spend so little time with spatial stimulants that they need our extra help and motivation to engage with technology.

Sensory System—Females tend to process more sensory data across the senses. They tend to see better (in certain kinds of light), hear better, use their sense of smell better, and take in more tactile information.

And this means—Girls' heightened sensory processing may well be another piece of the puzzle regarding why girls include more sensory detail in their writing and conversation. They will generally use more varied color in their artwork. They will generally use more sensory words to make their point than boys do. Boys are more likely than girls to have a difficult time hearing certain ranges of sound, especially from their usual self-selected seat in the back of the room! They may seem to be listening to directions, but in fact may not be hearing them as well as we think.

Mother Nature is providential. She gives us twelve years to develop a love for our children before turning them into teenagers.

—William Galvin

Chemical Differences

There are differences in the types and amounts of hormones and neurotransmitters that affect how boys and girls learn and interact. We've mentioned some of these. Let's now look more closely at them.

Testosterone—Testosterone is the male sex and aggression hormone, responsible for the architecture of the male system before birth and for the male's increased aggression, competitiveness, self-assertion, and self-reliance throughout life. Male testosterone levels rise when males "win" and decline when males "lose." Female testosterone levels, always lower than males, remain basically constant and are not as subject to fluctuations brought about by winning or losing.

> *And this means*—healthy competition in the classroom will help motivate boys. Research has shown that boys tend to score better on tests at times when testosterone levels are high, and levels rise during competition. Using games that provide all students a chance to succeed, even if they are competing against themselves and "beating themselves" at a task, can be very productive. And although girls' testosterone levels don't fluctuate as boys' do, research shows that girls generally gain self-confidence from active, healthy competition. Keep in mind: boys are also competing with each other in their social lives, to attain hierarchical status and to be attractive to girls. Beginning with puberty, girls are competing to attract males who will make the best partners, so as to ultimately create the best offspring. This is not a conscious process; although the boys and girls you teach are aware that they like each other and want to connect, they are generally unaware of the biological imperatives at work within them.

Estrogen—Estrogen is not one hormone but a group of hormones, often collectively identified as the female sex hormone. Although estrogens are present in both males and females, they are usually present at significantly higher levels in girls and women. They promote the development of female secondary sex characteristics. Researchers have found that estrogen levels may affect aggressive tendencies in females, and levels may be affected by seasonal variations, such as the amount of daylight. Further, girls with greater amounts of body fat may be subject to earlier onset of puberty, as the body believes it is more prepared for reproduction because of increased hormone levels.

> *And this means*—for girls who are overweight, puberty may come quite early, even at the age of eight or nine, bringing with it increased levels of estrogen and the potential for more volatile mood swings and more aggressive behavior. As the outward signs of puberty become noticeable, the changes to the brain that accompany puberty are also beginning. These changes have a significant impact on behavior and performance for girls, beginning as early as third or fourth grade and continuing through middle school and into high school.

Serotonin—Serotonin is a neurotransmitter known as a "feel-good" chemical. It affects mood and anxiety, and helps us relax and cool off during times of conflict. Girls' serotonin level tend to be about 30 percent higher than that of boys, making them less apt to rely on a fight response when in a conflict, although the emotional turmoil of adolescence can cause them to become involved in more conflicts than they did as younger children or will as they get older. Once angered, boys have less access to serotonin to help them manage their anger. Dr. Bruce Perry has studied neurotransmitters and found them to be very responsive to environmental stimuli. He reports that "kindness can be physically calming," helping increase serotonin levels.

> *And this means*—boys will have less serotonin in their system to help them calm down and de-escalate volatile situations. Although girls generally process serotonin more efficiently, they are responding from a revved up emotional system during adolescence too. An intervention by a calm, kind, supportive adult will be more helpful than one from an adult who engages in a power struggle that can escalate a boy's fight response or a girl's emotional response.

Dopamine—Dopamine is a neurotransmitter that stimulates motivation and pleasure circuits in the brain of both boys and girls. It is critical to the way the brain controls our movements. Not enough dopamine? We can't move or control our movements well. Too much dopamine? We can become subject to uncontrollable or subconscious movements (pencil tapping, leg jiggling, inability to sit still, even seriously uncontrolled involuntary motor movements). Dopamine also controls the flow of information between areas of the brain, especially when it is engaged in memory, attention, and problem-solving tasks.

And this means—in boys who are "revved up" with dopamine, accompanying lower levels of serotonin can make it harder for them to calm their impulses than it is for girls. Their increased stimulation may actually tend to stimulate them more, causing them to spiral more and more out of control. A balance must be found in the classroom to help students get a "dopamine rush" from learning, but in an environment that provides enough structure to manage enthusiasm.

Oxytocin—Oxytocin is often referred to as the "tend and befriend" hormone and is related to social recognition and bonding. Researchers have shown it to be involved in the formation of trust between people. Females have significantly higher levels of oxytocin in their systems than males throughout life. Oxytocin promotes the development and maintenance of relationships, and females are biologically driven to maintain relationships, even ones that are sometimes best let go.

And this means—girls will be motivated by their chemical system to establish and maintain relationships with teachers and peers, and will behave in ways meant to meet that need, including pleasing the teacher, their parents, and their friends. Boys are less chemically driven to establish and maintain these relationships prima facie, and may not see their behavior as having as much direct connection to their relationships with the teacher and their peers. During adolescence, for both boys and girls, peer connection is vitally important, and the need to establish and maintain relationships can override the need to perform well academically. Recognizing the importance of peer relationships and incorporating positive group activities into the curriculum will help students meet their needs and your expectations.

The Two Hemispheres

We each have only one brain, but that brain is divided right down the middle into right and left hemispheres. Research shows that each hemisphere appears to be specialized for some behaviors. The corpus callosum, which we discussed earlier, is a main communication link between the two hemispheres, and as with many brain functions, there are gender differences in how we use the two sides of our brain.

Left-hemisphere preference is more common in *girls.* The left brain

- Is connected to the right side of the body
- Processes information sequentially and analytically
- Generates spoken language

- Recognizes words and numbers (when the numbers are spoken as words)

- Responds more to external sensory stimuli, such as color and texture of fabric

- Constructs memories (including hyperbolic [exaggerated] memories)

- Does arithmetic functions—adding, subtracting, multiplying, dividing

- Seeks explanations for occurrence of events

Right-hemisphere preference is more common in *boys*. The right brain

- Is connected to the left side of the body

- Processes information abstractly and holistically

- Interprets language nonverbally

- Recognizes places, faces, objects, music

- Fantasizes abstractions (such as in science fiction and video game scenarios)

- Is less detailed and more concrete in recall

- Does relational and mathematical functions—for example algebra, geometry, trigonometry, calculus

- Organizes occurrences into spatial patterns

Although of course the brain functions in both hemispheres, the right and left hemisphere preference of boys and girls has important implications when we look at how our schools are designed. Most educators will admit that schools are designed to be more left-hemisphere friendly: they are structured environments with time periods and ringing bells, are organized around facts and rules, rely primarily on verbal processing, limit access to free space and movement, and require lots of multitasking.

Because this left-hemisphere-friendly environment naturally favors left-hemisphere preferences, girls are going to find school, in general, more comfortable than will many boys. Not surprisingly, schools report that 80 to 90 percent of their discipline problems are created by boys. Boys are not only biochemically more prone to "make a fuss" than girls but also quite often chafing against an environment that doesn't fit their right-hemisphere preference as learners.

If you would like a more comprehensive overview of the differences between the male and female brain, you might want to read *Boys and Girls Learn Differently!* and *The Wonder of Girls* (by Michael Gurian) and *The Minds of Boys* (by Michael Gurian and Kathy Stevens).

Looking at the Male-Female Brain Spectrum

Although the brains of adolescent boys and girls are different, it's important to remember that one boy's brain is also different from another boy's brain. The same is true of the girl's brain. Every individual's brain architecture falls somewhere on the male-female brain spectrum, a continuum from "the most male" to "the most female." What do we mean by that?

Researchers have identified what Michael Gurian has labeled "bridge brains," brains that fall in the middle of that spectrum. Bridge brains tend to have wiring whose structure more completely overlaps the typical male and female brain architecture than might an "average" male or female. Research conducted by the Amen Clinics (which have performed thirty-five thousand brain scans) in the United States and by Professor Simon Baron-Cohen at Cambridge in the United Kingdom has confirmed the wide spectrum of male and female brains, as well as the existence of males and females in the middle of that spectrum. According to Baron-Cohen's scans, for instance, approximately one in five females and one in seven males fall within the bridge-brain range. These bridge brains are most easily seen after puberty or in late adolescence, after the years of hormonal surges have nearly completed the development of the brain.

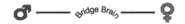

A teenage girl wired as a bridge brain might have a brain system inclined to process more like a male brain. These girls may enjoy activities that are very competitive and highly spatial, and that require a higher degree of risk tolerance—such as competitive sports or the debate or chess team. An adolescent boy bridge brain might find that he enjoys activities involving more verbal and emotional sensitivity and processing—such as theater, writing, or visual and performing arts.

It's important to be on the lookout for children, especially adolescents, who might think just a little differently than others of their gender. Bridge-brain boys and girls may find this period particularly stressful if they don't feel that they "fit in" with the prevailing "girl culture" or "boy culture." In this workbook, you'll find many ways to help all children, wherever they fit on the male-female brain spectrum.

Gender Difference: A Path to Success

Understanding that boys' and girls' brains are wired differently is just the beginning. Focusing on how those differences affect the classroom is the next step. In the rest of this workbook, we will focus on strategies designed to help you create a classroom that will meet the developmental needs of your students to ensure their success.

In the last decade, the Gurian Institute Training Division has worked throughout the United States and Canada in more than a thousand schools, public and private, coed and single-sex. This work has been utilized in classrooms by over twenty-five thousand teachers in the United States, Canada, and Australia. By helping teachers, administrators, parents, and others working with children understand the differences in how boys and girls learn, and by providing (and gathering from wise teachers) strategies that work, we assist schools in changing the way they do the business of education. Specifically, they are succeeding in closing achievement gaps, helping at-risk students, helping students with learning disabilities, and creating classroom stability.

Roosevelt Middle School: A Success Story

Roosevelt Middle School is in a large, urban school district and is 100 percent free lunch; it is 65 percent Hispanic, 25 percent white, 8 percent black, 2 percent other. The school has approximately nine hundred students in grades 6–8. In 2005, Roosevelt had a gender gap in reading achievement of 17 percent. The boys scored 55 percent satisfactory on the eighth-grade criterion-referenced test (CRT) for reading; the girls scored 72 percent. To address this gap, Roosevelt's principal, Marilyn Vrooman, began looking for strategies that would correct the problem and recommended piloting some gender work in classrooms. Teachers and parents agreed. Ms. Vrooman contacted the Gurian Institute Training Division and arranged for on-site training.

On the first day, trainers observed, took notes, and studied behavior. On the second day, they conducted an all-day in-service for faculty and administration. After the training, Roosevelt's teachers were charged up again. The school purchased books (*The Minds of Boys, The Wonder of Girls,* and *Boys and Girls Learn Differently!*) for each teacher as resource material, and they conducted book studies. The teachers realigned their classrooms to meet the needs of the genders and changed the materials used to teach. Responding to their training and reading, teachers realized that boys do not like "touchy-feely stuff" as much as girls. They like nonfiction, cars, action. Keeping totally within the state standards for each class, the teachers used different materials, and the boys took off.

At Roosevelt, somewhat atypically, fights between girls were four times more frequent than fights between boys. In a typical year, there would be one hundred girl fights and twenty-five boy fights (mostly gang related). In the year following the training, there were fewer than thirty fighting incidents, involving girls less often than boys. At the end of the year, boys scored 71 percent satisfactory on the reading CRT, and the girls scored 80 percent, narrowing the achievement gap to 9 percent in one year and improving performance for both the girls and the boys.

Roosevelt celebrates student achievement every day. For the first time in four years, the school is off the state's "at risk" list. Ms. Vrooman again scheduled a two-day training with her faculty and administration in 2006 and 2007, providing support and encouragement to continue the success they have initiated.

Schools and teachers who use the strategies suggested in this book have provided us with success data in these quantitative areas:

- Test scores

- Grades

- Discipline referrals

For this workbook, we've gathered field-tested strategies and best practices, Web sites, resources, and in-class projects and tools that you can begin to use today. Everything we recommend works for both boys and girls, hindering neither. Many of these strategies and practices grow from research and from teachers' wisdom of practice that target boys or girls specifically, but we haven't included (and never support) any practice that would be detrimental to either boys or girls.

The improvement at Roosevelt Middle School is one example of the success that can occur when teachers and schools understand how boys and girls learn differently, and provide training and resources to help teachers implement effective strategies consistent with that knowledge. Every teacher at Roosevelt knows that one group of strategies is not the only cause of statistical gains in test scores. Teachers are constantly testing many innovations, and many variables can improve learning. At the same time, Roosevelt teachers were happy to see rewards for their focus on gender-based learning differences. By visiting the Gurian Institute Web site (www.gurianinstitute.com), you can read more stories of success and learn more about how teachers and schools are improving performance and helping kids excel.

———————

Now we hope you'll enjoy the remaining chapters of this book, which show you how to implement strategies like those at Roosevelt in your own secondary classroom right now. We hope, too, that what you read here will resonate with your life experience as a teacher and make you say, perhaps a little more often than you did before, "I sure love teaching these kids."

Maximizing the Brain-Body Connection

2

Moving Through the Curriculum

Learning is an active process. We learn by doing. Only knowledge that is used sticks in your mind.

—Dale Carnegie

STUDENTS typically get to move around between classes every fifty minutes or so, but for many of them, that's physically, neurally, and biochemically inadequate. Their brains would work better if they moved more. The adolescent body is not designed to sit in a chair for six hours a day. In today's classrooms, sitting is what students do the most. Quite often, teachers "teach to the students' heads," and everything from the shoulders down gets ignored in the learning process. This tendency in schools can be dealt with first by reframing learning toward brain-friendly movement innovations, then focusing on specific boy-girl needs in movement, then altering the classroom in subtle but significant ways.

As you begin this chapter, please know that we as authors and practitioners are aware of how much content you have to teach—we will provide, not pie-in-the-sky movement and hands-on interactive projects that would distract from good learning, but instead, body-brain connection activities that can improve both academic performance and behavior.

The Importance of Physical Movement in Learning

There are many links between the body and the brain. Cells and chemicals throughout the body are stimulated when the body moves. When learning is paired with movement, we anchor learning in the body through procedural memory. When the body learns a concept, the brain is less likely to forget it. This is especially true for boys.

Although movement is important for all students, boys generally need more movement while learning than do girls. For many adolescent boys, movement is necessary at intervals for keeping the brain stimulated and controlling impulsive behavior. The increased blood flow and oxygen to the brain, along with the release of neurotransmitters, helps these students learn concepts and procedures better, retain them longer, and cause less of a distraction in the classroom with unfocused activity.

Generally speaking, elementary school classrooms offer more movement opportunities than secondary school classrooms. Certainly, younger students' neurological systems are less mature and attention spans are shorter—they just cannot sit as long as older students can, no matter how firmly the teacher directs them to do so. Primary teachers have no choice but to let students get up and do jumping jacks or change activities frequently. If they don't, the little ones will be rolling around on the floor and poking each other.

Although older students may often appear to tolerate the "sit-n-git" lecture, appearances can be very misleading. Students who are sitting quietly in their seats may be somewhere else entirely in their minds. Boys' brains might go to a biological rest state and be mentally absent during an entire class. Girls' brains may not go into as deep a rest or "zoned out" state, but they can be absent as they mentally wander to someplace far from the classroom. Both of these occurrences are much more likely when a teacher stands in front of the class and lectures for an entire class period. Just because we *can* get students to sit at their desks for the entire period does not mean that we *should.*

Among the many reasons movement is good for both the adolescent body and mind, for both boys and girls, is this one: our teenagers today are more sedentary than those living in any other period in history. This state of contemporary life has led to an epidemic of overweight children. More hidden is the effect on learning brains. When you utilize strategies to integrate more movement into your classroom, you will be helping the learning brains of your students in some very profound ways—and you will be rescuing this generation of children from an epidemic of sedentary life that is not a good fit with adolescent hormones or development.

Synaptic connections. During adolescent development, many neural pathways between brain cells do not form except through physical engagement. And remember, during adolescence there are significant numbers of new dendrites, creating the potential for many new neural pathways and making this a window of opportunity we can't afford to ignore.

Motor control. During adolescence, the growing brain "prunes" cells to shed the connections that are not being utilized. If the brain doesn't get to "move around" through physical activity during adolescence, it may not develop the healthy habits needed to promote an overall healthy lifestyle throughout life.

Points to Ponder Jar

Use a "Points to Ponder" jar to stop periodically and shift gears—perhaps when you can sense that the energy level of your students is really low, when you want to reengage the group before covering some important content, or when you just want to give everyone a break! Start with these and add your own (and get your students to contribute):

- How do they get deer to cross at those little yellow signs?
- Do Lipton Tea employees get to take coffee breaks?
- How can you have a "civil" war?

You get the idea. Just pull a slip of paper with a Point to Ponder from the jar on your desk at some unexpected moment. Most of these will result in everyone having a good laugh—another very positive thing for the learning brain, as laughter releases endorphins, which elicit a sense of well-being. Following this brain break, it will be easier for both boys and girls to refocus on the content you are delivering.

Brain integration. Movement, especially cross-lateral (left and right) movement, aids in the healthy development and integration of both hemispheres. This can be especially helpful to adolescents as they navigate the developmental waters of connecting thinking and feeling areas of the brain.

Attention and reward. Certain neurotransmitters, such as dopamine, are stimulated by physical activity and novelty; movement thus helps the brain keep boredom states at bay and helps control impulsive acting out (thereby improving classroom behavior).

Circulation and respiration. Increasing blood flow and oxygen to the brain increases the brain's ability to pay attention, solve problems, and retain information. An alert and engaged brain uses nearly 50 percent of the oxygen in the body to stay alert and engaged.

Stress. Negative stress, or distress, reduces the number of new neurons that a brain generates each day. Physical movement decreases the likelihood of distress, while also reducing aggression, avoidance, and apprehension about learning. Sometimes movement activities result in spontaneous laughter. Laughter not only mitigates potentially harmful chemicals but also promotes the release of endorphins in the brain, which help students enjoy learning. Note: research has shown that girls are more subject to depression during adolescence, so mitigating stress can help promote better mental health for girls.

Wisdom of Practice

Teachers working across all content areas are recognizing the importance of getting their students moving, both in body and mind. The following examples from creative teachers are just a few ways of making this strategy come to life in the classroom.

At Cherry Creek PREP Alternative High School, teachers teach lessons on anger management, conflict resolution, and communication modes. After each lesson, students are given different scenarios to read and then act out. Groups act out a negative example (how *not* to handle the situation) and then an example of what to do using the skills they have learned.

Seventh-grade science teacher Leonard Jones makes movement a regular part of his classroom routine. After teaching a new concept, Leonard has his students take on various roles and use pantomime to demonstrate their understanding. For example, Leonard's students each play a part of a cell and demonstrate the various functions.

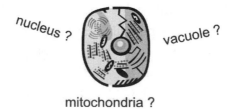

Tracy Brennan, International Baccalaureate English teacher, helps her students develop a deeper understanding of Shakespeare's *Hamlet* and *Macbeth* by having them act out various scenes. Even literature not written in the dramatic genre is interpreted through dramatic enactments. She has found this to increase retention of content among her students.

What are some negative stressors in your school environment that might be having an effect on your boys and your girls specifically? Brainstorm with your students. Hear what they have to say. Then teach them the functions of the brain we are now looking at that pertain to body-brain connections and movement. See if their eyes light up when you ask them to come up with safe, reasonable ways of not only minimizing negative stressors but also enjoying more movement in your classroom during learning.

History teacher Mary Lott has students create a time line across the classroom. Mary tapes historical events to each student's back so that the students cannot see which historical event they represent. Without talking, students work together to put themselves in chronological order along the time line. They can then take the signs off their backs, check their accuracy, and share with the rest of the class something important about their event.

Special education teacher Julianne Pion does brain integration activities with her students daily. Students trace figure eights on paper with a crayon and in the air with their arm and head as they cross their body's midline. She reports that parents and teachers alike have noted significant increases in eye tracking, upper body strength, motor control, balance, flexibility, and coordination. Julianne's students with severe disabilities have shown remarkable improvements in their ability to write from left to right, stay within the lines, and produce smaller, more uniform letters on the page.

Chris Mischke and Ginny Vidulich team-teach middle school language arts and social studies. Their students never know for sure how the desks will be arranged, and the routine is changed regularly to create novelty. Chris and Ginny break up teacher-led instruction by alternating seven- or eight-minute chunks of direct instruction with interactive activities that allow students to move and socially engage with one another.

Common Teacher Questions and Concerns

Utilizing more movement for learning entails something of a shift in teaching style. Here are some of the questions teachers have asked us and one another—and here are some answers.

"Is there enough room in my classroom for movement?"

Many of the middle and high school classrooms we visit are pretty cramped: considering the students' desks and chairs, the teacher's desk and chair, bookcases, and educational materials, not to mention book bags, gym bags, and purses, space can be at a real premium! But even in tight spaces, we've seen teachers do amazing things with movement.

Something to keep in mind: although teachers often worry about boys being squeezed into too little space, space can be a problem for girls too. They may find the proximity of classmates encouraging of their desire to socialize, and because they are more relationship driven, the motivation to connect may override the need to stay focused on the teacher.

If you work in an open-space school, you have a different kind of problem. You may feel limited by your proximity to other classes and the need to stay fairly quiet, something teenagers in general can find tough to do.

"Interactive activities that require you to move around and get out of your seat make learning more fun."

—10th grade girl

"There should be more windows in our school and MUCH less bookwork."

—10th grade girl

"I think that it would be easier on people if they did not have to come in and sit at a desk day after day."

—8th grade boy

"School should have more hands-on, group work and activities to help you learn faster."

—6th grade girl

"School should do more outdoor activities and more games instead of worksheets and textbooks."

—6th grade girl

Note that four of these five comments are from girls— suggesting that girls like and benefit from movement every bit as much as boys!

TRY THIS Pass It Back

Try this strategy game next time you are reviewing for a quiz in your cramped classroom.

Create a fill-in-the-blank sheet of statements using the material to be covered on the quiz (or create a list of math problems, words that must be matched with definitions, and so on, as this activity can be adapted to fit any content area). Have each row of desks be a team. Ask student to put away all their materials except for a pen or pencil. Hand the first person in each row a game sheet, face down, and tell them not to turn it over until you say "Go." You will give the class a designated number of minutes to completely fill in the blanks on the game sheet. The first team done will raise their hands and then wait for the remaining teams to finish, each team raising their hands as they finish.

When you say "Go," the person in the front seat turns over the game sheet, fills in a blank (you can determine whether they must go in order or can start anywhere on the sheet), then passes it over his or her head to the person in the next seat. When the sheet gets to the end of the row, the last person brings it back to the front, and the first person goes again until all blanks are filled in. Each team member can fill in a new blank space or correct an answer already given that he or she believes to be wrong. After all teams are finished, go over the answers.

In this case, explore other options, such as the gymnasium, stage, cafeteria, or break-out space.

You can also consider taking the learning outdoors. Playgrounds, playing fields, and campus centers (weather permitting) allow for even greater movement with less concern about noise. An added benefit: there are many documented health benefits to outdoor light. Estrogen levels in adolescent girls are believed to be affected by the length of day and amount of natural light to which they are exposed. This information has a lot of import in a place like Minneapolis, Minnesota, where students receive in the winter, on average, only thirty minutes of natural outdoor light a day. Greater exposure to natural light decreases stress and depression and increases academic performance. It also helps with the processing of calcium so that it's available for developmental needs.

Further, adolescents need plenty of time outdoors to allow the visual cortex to develop properly. It is outside where young people can hone the visual skills needed to judge and accurately estimate depth and distances. Unfortunately, by middle school and high school, many students do not go

Here's an example of a Pass It Back game you could try with a history or government class. You can also create your own list using names from current events.

Draw a line to match a name in the left column with information in the right column

Clara Barton	Moses of her people
George Armstrong Custer	Pioneer of women's rights
Harriet Tubman	16th president of the United States
Samuel L. Clemens	Founder of the Red Cross
Dred Scott	1st black professional baseball player
Abraham Lincoln	1st president of the United States
Susan B. Anthony	Mark Twain
George Washington	Slave who sued for his freedom
Jackie Robinson	General in the Battle of the Little Big Horn

outside at all during the course of their school day, as they no longer have an outdoor recess, and physical education may not be one of their electives. More unfortunately, many school buildings were built with a mission of saving money on heating and cooling, so they contain classrooms with no windows to let in natural light. These trends can be counterproductive to adolescent learning, as Mary Rivkin, author of *The Great Outdoors: Restoring Student's Right to Play Outside,* has confirmed in her research: students learn certain things better in the outdoors because that is where most of our human genetics for learning evolved.

"When am I going to find time in the day for movement activities?"
We know there is never enough time in a typical forty- to fifty-five-minute class period to get to all the content you feel pressured to cover. You may even find yourself limiting class discussion or students' questions in an effort to get through a lesson plan. How can you now add movement activities?!

One answer lies in your defining the purpose of the movement activity you are considering. Is the purpose of the movement simply to change the

"Within a class period, I will pick a time, somewhere about half-way through the hour, to stop whatever is going on and make all the students get up and move around. They may use this time to socialize, sharpen a pencil, turn paperwork in, or just walk around the classroom. I give them a set amount of time so they can monitor themselves; at the end of the set time they settle down and are back on task, refocused, and ready to finish out the hour."
—Sherri Becker, South Lake Middle School

"I give math quizzes by stations sometimes. I place one question at each of, say, ten stations, and the students get an answer sheet numbered one through ten. If I have twenty students, then two at a time go to each station; when I signal (with a whistle or some other device) they move to the next station. Some students will start with 1 and go through 10. Some will start with 4, continue through 10, then go to 1 through 3. When the last whistle blows, everyone returns to their seats. Some teachers have asked me if I worry about the kids cheating. Not really. The girls do find it harder not to talk, so I have to remind them more often to be silent—they don't want to cheat, they just want to talk! But they all enjoy the time out of their seats and know if they abuse the opportunity they'll be sitting taking their quiz in the old fashioned way."

—Anna Walters, middle school math and science teacher

physical state—to increase oxygen, blood flow, and heart rate—which will quickly reenergize or relax the body and brain for learning? If this is the case, the activity you choose (many are provided at the end of the chapter) can be kept pretty brief, and doesn't require of a lot of set-up, transitions, or materials. These activities can be done on the spot and can be sprinkled in as you see that your students need them.

If you are planning to use a movement activity to teach, practice, review, or assess the content that you are delivering, there is no need to separate movement from content. This is not about movement *or* reading, movement *or* science, but rather movement *and* reading, movement *and* science. Check out the example in the sidebar.

"Won't I lose control of the class?"

This is a common concern of many teachers. Fortunately, as teachers put movement activities into their classrooms, they quickly notice (as do the students) the difference between unproductive, off-task noise and the noise that is generated by students fully engaged in an exciting task. Also remember that during more sedentary classroom activities, students could be off task or daydreaming and you may simply be less likely to notice! Movement itself is not any more "distracting" than sedentary learning—and it is a more overt way of learning, so you can control it better with your own observation and authority.

Before starting movement activities with your class, allow plenty of time to discuss and rehearse the procedural expectations. Practice how

---

A Principal's Observations

"In my journal notes what I was finding was that the teachers were constantly asking the boys to be quiet or be still yet the boys were often completing their assignments and actually teaching each other. I told the teachers that I also found that in classes I visited where the girls were working in groups, the girls were allowed to go on for several minutes being off task while they quietly talked. The problem I found was the *quietly talking* rarely was because the girls were talking about an assignment but what the girls would "discuss" were topics such as nail polish color, who they talked to on the phone the day before, what boy they liked, etc. Once I drew the teacher's attention to my journal notes, they realized that quite often the boys were indeed staying on task and completing work whereas the girls (although a great deal quieter) were having to be redirected to complete assigned work."

—Yvette Keel, middle school principal

students can move safely in the classroom and how they can stop the activity quickly and focus back on you when necessary. The time spent up front will be well worth it and will ensure a more enjoyable experience for all.

"The principal won't think we're learning unless the students are sitting quietly at their desks."

Many principals are against physical movement until they participate in training or do research on how the brain learns and on how boys and girls learn differently. If you can, get your principal to see the brain research and action research that is available. Let him or her see how movement improves the learning of both boys and girls, in their own ways.

If the principal is cautious, you might provide him or her with your answers to the questions that follow. These can be your personal "proof," beyond the research, that you are succeeding or poised to succeed in your new innovations.

1. Are the students clear about what they should know and be able to do as a result of this lesson?

2. How is the movement activity helping students acquire, rehearse, or review the concept or skill?

3. Is the noise and movement directly related to the teaching and learning activities (that is, are the students on task or off task)?

4. What evidence do I have that students are mastering the concepts or skills?

5. What evidence do I have that students are motivated and engaged in the learning process?

> *Learning is experience. Everything else is just information.*
> —Albert Einstein

Practical Ideas for Your Classroom

Although we have tried to be fairly comprehensive in our list of movement activities, no such list could ever be exhaustive. Just as your curriculum will vary from state to state and grade to grade, so too will your individual teacher and student needs and interests. Fortunately, teachers are incredibly creative individuals who find new and better ways of doing things every day. Look to each other as resources! Sharing ideas with other teachers at department or faculty meetings, on an "Ideas" bulletin board in the lounge, or via online blog sites will most certainly yield a multitude of new ideas to complement the curriculum in every subject and at every grade. Always remember, if you create a great new brain break or any activity, send it in to

"My history teacher sometimes uses activities like a tug-of-war (to represent French involvement in the US revolution), or a demo involving eating clam chowder to show cultural and climate differences."

—*10th grade boy*

"I like it when lessons are made into a game. I learn more and remember more."

—*6th grade girl*

us at www.gurianinstitute.com. Include your name, your school, and your location. If we feature it in the future, we will make sure to give you and your colleagues credit.

As you try out the following ideas, think about the information you have learned about the brains of boys and girls, and ask, "How will this activity help the boys?" "How will this activity help the girls?" You might be intrigued by your own answers—especially as they grow from your own practice and innovation.

Quick "Anytime" Brain Breaks

Keep this list of brain breaks handy and be ready to use them whenever you detect low energy, or just prior to introducing an important concept or skill. You and your students will reenergize body and brain.

Stretch!   Have students roll their shoulders, stretch their necks from side to side, lean over and touch the floor—anything to wake up their bodies and get the blood flowing again.

Cross-Laterals   These activities get both sides of the brain talking to one another. Have students pat their right ear, shoulder, or elbow with their left hand and vice versa. Cross-laterals also include marching in place while patting opposite knees or heels. (This kind of activity helps develop neural pathways that will offset some of the physical clumsiness that seems to plague both male and female adolescents.)

Hand Fidgets   Provide a variety of "fidgets," small items with interesting textures—for example, stress balls, bean bags, Koosh balls, gel-filled toys, smooth stones, rubber tubing, and strips of Velcro. Allow students to get a fidget if they need one. This is especially helpful to boys, who find it more difficult to keep still while doing seat work. Girls, due to their heightened sensory intake, will enjoy the textures of the various fidgets. Note: we've heard from high school boys who carry a stress ball in their book bag—they've figured out that it helps when they have to sit!

Deep Breathing   Have students stand up and take deep breaths, exhaling slowly. Students can put their hands on their chests to feel the intake and release of their breath. Have students rise up on their tiptoes as they inhale and go back down to flat feet as they exhale. Using some slow music with this activity is a plus.

Standing Up   If you are round-robin reading or reviewing for a test, consider conducting the activity standing up. Caution: don't make students stand "at attention," as this can cause problems similar to those related to having to sit still. Allow modest movement as students stand, as long as they are not being distracting to their classmates.

Do the Wave Charge the group up by having them do "the wave" or a silent shout. They stand up, stretch their arms high and shout, "Whooo!" in a wavelike pattern across the classroom. Have them send the wave back. Use this activity as a way for your students to give a group response to a question, saying "Yesssssss" or "Nooooooo."

Gotcha! In circle groups, have students put their left hand, palm up, in front of the person to their left. Then have them extend their right index finger and place it in the palm of the hand of the person on their right. When you say "Go!" students try to do two things: pull their right finger away from the person on their right and try to grab the finger of the person on their left.

Mirror Image Have each student face a partner. One partner moves slowly and carefully, while the other partner mirrors his or her movements. Make it more difficult by having one partner do several movements with the other partner just watching. Then the second partner can try to repeat the movements. Try pairing the students up boy-boy, girl-girl, and boy-girl. Is there a difference in how the activity "goes" depending on the gender pairing?

Making Contact Establish a snapping, clapping, slapping rhythm for the group to follow. Musical accompaniment makes it more fun. Everyone faces a partner and executes the rhythm. Then the leader calls out various commands, such as foot-to-foot, and the partners put their feet together as they continue their snap-clap-slap rhythm. The leader continues with commands such as head-to-head, back-to-back, and side-to-side, and students follow the commands while maintaining their snap-clap-slap rhythm.

Adaptable for Any Subject Area

Activities that encourage the boys to engage their verbal processing resources are definitely a plus to continue developing literacy skills. Having girls engage their spatial resources gets them to "exercise" less used resources that will become increasingly important as they move into more abstract content and higher math.

Scavenger Hunts Have students move about the classroom or school to document different items and their association with the concept being learned. For example, when studying the concept of leadership, students might find pictures, posters, slogans, and books that connect to the leadership theme. What evidence can students find in the school regarding rules, policies, laws, or constitutional rights? What architectural design principles can be noted in the construction of the school building? How many different geometric shapes can be found in the construction of the school building?

Musical Chairs   Play musical chairs with a twist. Instead of eliminating the student left standing, he or she answers a question about the content you are teaching. The game continues so that many students get to answer a question. (Yes, adolescents still enjoy playing a game of musical chairs from time to time—and if they spend a lot of the time laughing, think of all those positive endorphins!)

Walking Review   Have each student take a walk with a partner around the school building. During his or her walk, the students reviews what they just learned or what is going to be on the upcoming test.

> One middle school teacher we worked with did this so often and the kids enjoyed it so much that they started keeping track of how many miles they walked each week, month, and semester. At the end of the semester and again at the end of the year, they put a map of their city up on the wall, put a piece of yarn around a push pin, and drew a circle for the number of miles away from the school they would have been if they had walked their miles in a straight line. It made for some really interesting discussion!

Ball Toss Review   For review, have students sit in a circle and pass a ball or a beanbag. Ask a review question and toss the object. The student who catches it answers the question and throws it to someone else. This continues with the teacher asking review questions and the students passing so that everyone gets a chance. Make this activity even more brain friendly and have the students try using just one hand, then the opposite hand when both throwing and catching the item. Do you see a difference in skill level between the boys and girls? Does that change as you have them use different strategies for catching and throwing?

Finger Spelling   Teach students the alphabet in sign and have them practice their content vocabulary with finger spelling. This can be especially helpful in foreign language classes where students are learning to spell the words.

Who's Got Talent?   Divide students into small groups. Identify several key words, skills, or concepts from the lesson. Have teams incorporate the concepts into a song-and-dance routine that they perform for the class. Do you find a gender difference in how students respond to this strategy? Try offering two strategies to choose from—this one and the next, Attack of the Stickies, and use single-gender groupings. Is there a difference between which activity is selected by the boy and girl groups?

Attack of the Stickies   Divide students up into four or five different groups and give each group a pad of sticky notes, each of a different color. Have them brainstorm a list of questions about an upcoming topic of study and write each question on a sticky note. As each question is generated, have them run up to a designated surface and post their sticky, return to the group, and repeat for as many questions as they can think of.

Vote with Your Feet   Designate opposite corners of the room as "strongly agree" and "strongly disagree." Provide students with statements about which they can formulate an opinion. This could be based on a reading passage in English class or an ethical question in science or social studies. Have students move to one of the corners or somewhere in between, depending on their level of agreement. Have the students in the corners defend their position to other students and try to talk the students in the middle into coming to their corner. Use a timer to keep anyone from monopolizing the time.

Specifically for Language Arts

Stimulating the neural connections between the spatial right brain and the verbal left brain is a key to promoting literacy performance for boys. These types of activities may help girls focus on their generally less preferred visual-spatial right-brain resources, meaning that all children benefit from increased activity. Following are some ways to make language arts learning fun. When we're having fun, our "chemical plant" responds in healthy ways!

How Can You Move?   Give half your students a red index card with a verb on it. Give the other half a blue index card with an adverb on it. Have students find a partner so that every pair of students has a verb and an adverb. Cue music and ask students to move in the manner specified by their cards—skip slowly, walk quickly, dance gracefully, and so on. Have some pairs demonstrate for the group. Observation note: Do you see any difference in how the girls and boys respond to the movements they have been asked to do? Do you hear any boys saying they aren't going to "dance gracefully"? You might see signs of socialization and stereotyping that children bring with them from their world away from school.

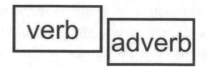

Sentence Strings   This activity can teach complex sentence structure and grammar. Put students in groups of four or five. Give each group an envelope that contains a collection of words and punctuation marks on index cards. Have students spread their cards out on the floor to make the longest, most complex (yet grammatically correct) sentence possible. If they are missing a word or a punctuation mark, they can negotiate a trade with another group.

Back on the Job   Have one student write a vocabulary word with his or her finger on another student's back. The student tries to figure out what the word is and then define it.

Word Charades   Without talking, students act out vocabulary words, and other students try to guess what they are. Note: teachers report that this can be real challenge for girls—who often find it frustrating not to be able to use language during an activity.

Word Games   Give each student a word on a laminated card. Have students close their eyes and mix themselves up. Have them put themselves in order as quickly as possible to create a sensible sentence—without talking. If the words are content-area specific, this activity can serve as a preview or review of concepts from across the curriculum, in addition to practice with grammar and sentence structure.

Specifically for Mathematics

Taking math off the page and into objects and manipulatives can help both genders. One way it helps girls has to do with their future: many girls will join professions that require spatial functioning, which they may have used less during elementary school than did many of the boys, having relied mainly on their own strong suit, verbal skills. Now, beefing up and practicing spatial skills can help girls develop resources for dealing with higher math concepts in algebra and geometry that will also help them in professional life.

Math Mania   Practice order of operations concepts and computations with dice. Roll several dice and display the numbers on the board. Have

students work in groups to combine the numbers using all four operations in various orders to generate several different answers. After an allotted amount of time, have the student groups demonstrate the answers they generated for the class with hops (for the hundreds place), jumping jacks (for the tens place), toe touches (for the ones place). Have students write their properly annotated number sentences on the board.

Olympic Math   Reinforce the order of operations by giving students a target number and then having them use the order of operations to combine twenty playing cards in as many different ways as possible to reach the targeted number. Have them form the numbers in the equations with their bodies.

Multiples in Motion   Practice multiples and factors of numbers by clapping and snapping! Give students a number and ask them to count from one to twenty by that number. Here's the trick: students are to count by clapping and saying the numbers in their head. When they reach a multiple, they should snap and say the number out loud. For example, multiples of three would be *clap, clap, snap*-"three"; *clap, clap, snap*-"six"; and so on.

Human Number Line   Give each student a card with a number on it, either a positive or negative integer (for example −15 through +15, if you have thirty-one students). Hand them out randomly and see how quickly students can put themselves in order. A variation is to put a sticker on each student's back so that students don't know their own number. Have them work silently to properly order themselves. When adding and subtracting positive and negative numbers, have one student move up and down the human number line to solve the equation.

More Number Lines   Have students stand along a number line from 0 to 25 (up to the number of students in your class). Have all the even numbers jump forward, all the odd numbers jump back; have all the numbers divisible by three support their weight on three body parts; have all the numbers divisible by four use four body parts; and so on.

Are You Right?   Have students use their arms to create angles of different sizes. Have them work collaboratively with other students to create different two- and three-dimensional geometric shapes. How might they create a triangular prism?

Frequency Table   Have students "graph" themselves. Have students line up along an x-axis based on their month of birth, day of the week they were born, their age in years-months-days, and so on. For an extra challenge, have them organize themselves without talking. Once they are along the x-axis, have them form parallel lines based on their categories; ask them what they have formed.

> We use this activity a lot with middle school math classes, and find it interesting when we divide the students into gender groupings. The boys tend to hold up fingers or use other nonverbal cues and move themselves into position. The girls may use the same nonverbal cues, but they also tend to move each other into place along the graph line; they also find it hard to refrain from talking! We point out to teachers who are puzzled by the girls' moving each other around that the girls know each other's birthdays. They tend to know lots of each other's personal information, such as birthdays, favorite colors, clothing styles, and so on.

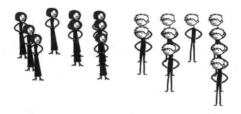

Time, Rate, and Distance   Have students figure out the relationship between time, rate, and distance with a stopwatch, beanbags, and a measured distance on the floor. Have students walk at different speeds along the designated line, dropping a beanbag every five seconds. Note: make this more interesting and have the students walk in different ways—like a runway model, an animal, a rock star, or something else of their own choosing. Are there differences in what the boys and girls choose?

How Many Letters on a Page?   Have students calculate the number of characters on a page from the newspaper. To do this, they take a one-by-one-inch square of paper and drop it on an open sheet of newspaper. They trace around the square of paper, and this becomes the "random sample." Have them count the characters within the square sample and then extrapolate out to calculate the number of characters on the whole sheet. Students can take multiple random samples to check their accuracy.

Specifically for Science

Science lends itself to "learning while moving" as well as, or better than, any other subject, to the benefit of both boys and girls. Making science fun can help engage those girls who may feel less comfortable with science than language arts. Here are a few science-related activities to add to your toolbox.

Solids, Liquids, and Gases   Designate a large area for students to move around freely. Then confine them to a smaller space to move around and then a very small space to move around. Discuss their ability to move (as molecules) in a large space (like a gas) versus a small space (like a solid).

A Periodic Review   Have students create a periodic table on asphalt with sidewalk chalk. It should be large enough for students to stand on the different elements. Draw elements from a hat and have the student who is standing on the element describe it. Have two elements join hands and discuss what they become when they are joined. Give clues and have students raise their hand if the clues apply to the element that they are standing on. Have students sit in groups around the perimeter of the periodic table. Have them send a "runner" to the element as their group's response to your questions.

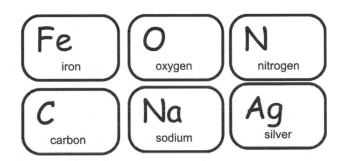

Dramatic Reenactments   Have students portray any scientific process through a mime performance set to music. For example, students could dramatize chemical changes, a life cycle process, physical interactions that result in changes in motion, the transport mechanisms in a cell (diffusion, osmosis, and active transport), and more.

Orbiting Planets   In an outdoor area or in the gym, set up cones to mark the sun and each of the planets. Have students line up along the orbit of one of the planets. Student groups can work together to demonstrate and explain the earth's place in the solar system and how the earth moves relative to the rest of the solar system. Have them demonstrate earth motions that control the length of days and timing of seasons, and then enact the phases of the earth's moon. Have students "travel" to different planets and moons in the solar system and explain the important properties and features of each. Students can also enact the formation and significance of comets, asteroids, and meteorites and demonstrate and describe the possible effects of collisions in space.

Viruses and Antibodies   Have students line up at one end of a hallway. Designate one student as the virus (tagger) and have that student stand in the middle of the hallway. The rest of the students are healthy cells. The healthy-cell students walk down the hallway toward and past the virus-cell student. The virus tries to tag as many students as possible by touching their shoulder. When healthy-cell students have been tagged, they then become virus cells and stay in the middle of the hallway to begin to tag other students on the next pass. Introduce "antibodies." These are students who cannot be tagged by the virus. Their job is to tag the virus-cell students so that those students again become normal cells. What happens to the proportion of students who are healthy cells and viruses before and after antibodies are introduced?

Cell Scrambler   On a playing field, mark several locations with the name of a part of a plant or animal cell (nucleus, vacuole, mitochondria, and so on). Give students clues about the functions of one of the cell parts. Students then "scramble" to the location that names the correct part of the cell. Gather together for a discussion and then try another scramble.

Push and Pull   Have pairs of students hold each other's hands and try pushing and pulling under different conditions, such as with one student sitting down while the other stands, with one student leaning back against a wall, or with one student in socks and the other in shoes. What are the variables that affect the application of force? Have students dramatize physical interactions that result in changes in motion, as well as potential and kinetic energy.

Unity and Diversity of Life   Have students write and perform a play with the following organisms as the main characters: virus, bacteria, fungi, protists, plants, and animals. The story line should illustrate each character's unique qualities, as well as the interdependence of the characters.

Physics Fun   Have groups of students work together, using their bodies and any materials that you may wish to provide them, to demonstrate kinetic energy, gravitational potential energy, thermal energy, elastic potential energy. Have them do it without words so that other students can guess the form of energy.

It's Electric!   Have students create parallel and series circuits on the floor with a rope and laminated cards for resistors, circuit breakers, bulbs, and so on. Have students walk around the circuit and discuss what is happening at each point of the circuit. Students can describe the properties of electrical conductivity as they walk the circuit.

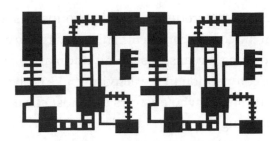

Time Marches On   Create a geological time line in your classroom. Have students represent important events throughout geological time by taking their place on the time line and providing an explanation about the geological event.

Specifically for Social Studies

Many teachers we work with have voiced concern that social studies is getting less attention in today's classrooms because it isn't as relevant to standardized tests. In tomorrow's (and today's!) world, however, the content of social studies becomes more and more important, as we prepare our students to compete and succeed in an ever-flattening world economy. Making social studies active and fun is a way to stress that it's important, while using it to reinforce literacy skills.

Clue Scramble   Identify specific places in your classroom or on the outdoor field. If you are studying different Spanish-speaking countries, for example, each place would be identified as a specific country. This activity is adaptable to a wide variety of content—simply label the area accordingly. Give students clues. When they think they know what you are referring to, they go to the specified place. If you are outdoors, they can move faster and more freely. Discuss what clues helped make the match. Give new clues and continue the game.

Compass Rose Run   Designate the four walls of the gym or other large area as the northern, southern, eastern, and western hemispheres. Provide clues that are specific to one of the hemispheres (clues related to the climate, geography, countries, and so on). Have students move in any way they choose to the correct hemisphere. Discuss the clues and the students' choices, then repeat.

Clue Sort   If you are studying continents, draw the outline of each continent on a piece of paper and put the papers on the floor in different places in the room. Hand out index cards with clues and information about the different continents. Have students work in groups to sort all their cards and place them on the correct continent. This activity can also be used with geographical landforms, oceans, historical landmarks, and more. If you want to add some competition to the activity, make each set of cards a different color so you can see who answers the most correctly, finishes first, and so on. Try arranging the groups as all boys, all girls, and coed. Do you see a difference in the way the groups function?

Time Travelers   Establish a time line in a large area. Give students different events and have them move in different ways to the place on the time line that the event took place.

Dramatic Reenactments   Have students act out different concepts or events (such as the basic elements of culture and social organization, the differences between economic systems, the stories and myths of various cultures, or how competition for resources leads to human conflict).

Storytelling   Awaken the lost art of storytelling in your classroom. Have students tell stories in the oral tradition about the cultures, religions, and politics that formed different societies. Make sure that they incorporate movement and body language into their storytelling to really bring the stories to life. As a twist, have the students become time travelers and take on a role—such as that of a rock star, a modern-day politician, or a news reporter—and report their story as if they had traveled back in time to visit the culture. Let students bring in costumes.

Finding Your Place in the World   Have students practice longitude and latitude by going onto the basketball court and figuring out what the lines on the court might equal in terms of degrees latitude or longitude. For example, the midcourt line would probably be the equator. Using estimation in the available space, can students place themselves at different coordinates? Where is the Tropic of Cancer?

Dance Through the Ages   Have students choreograph a dance that illustrates important concepts you're teaching. For example, students could portray through dance how the roles of people have changed over the course of the history, as related to gender, social class, caste, age, and so on. Students can also demonstrate various forms of dance, theater, and music that societies have used to express religious and philosophical beliefs. Note: this can be really interesting in a coed class—watch and see if you encounter any stereotypical responses by the girls or the boys in terms of their willingness to participate in this activity.

WRAPPING UP THE MAIN IDEAS

- Providing movement opportunities in the classroom is critical for adolescent brain development.

- Movement increases blood flow and oxygen to the brain, and releases a number of neurotransmitters that are helpful to learning.

- Adolescent brain and body development causes both boys and girls to be physically, mentally, and emotionally "clumsy," in gender-specific ways.

- Movement increases focus and motivation and improves memory for both boys and girls, in their own ways.

- Students often learn best by doing, and for boys, the physical movement involved in "doing" can keep them out of zone-out and brain-rest states.

- Movement can be used to energize, relax, focus attention, and facilitate transitions.

- Music that is upbeat will increase the heart rate, give students an adrenaline boost, and encourage more energized movement. Music that is slow and soft will help students slow down.

- Movement opportunities can be integrated across content areas so that students are learning while they're moving—for girls this can be especially helpful in science and technology areas.

- Teachers must take classroom management issues into consideration up front. Good planning and proper preparation with students will ensure that movement activities are successful and enjoyable for all.

Movement is about living and living is about learning.
—Eric Jensen

An active mind cannot exist in an inactive body.
—General George S. Patton

Creating a New Playbook

Using More Visual-Spatial Strategies in Your Classroom

3

Golf is deceptively simple and endlessly complicated; it satisfies the soul and frustrates the intellect. It is at the same time rewarding and maddening—and it is without a doubt the greatest game mankind has ever invented.

—Arnold Palmer

ARNOLD Palmer is talking about golf, but you can probably find a similar quotation from a maestro of any game—whether an aggressive one like football or soccer; a slower-paced physical game, such as bowling; or even a board game like chess or backgammon. What makes a master or the girl or boy in your class so love the game in which he or she is involved? How did these individuals get to the point where they could master the game? Where did they begin their path of mastery?

In any game, one begins the journey toward mastery when one moves from random and sporadic learning and activity to a specific plan of action. One day, as an adolescent, Arnold Palmer made an internal decision to try to master the game—and thus himself. He set out to develop a plan, sought out mentors (coaches), and practiced his craft. He and his mentors developed a playbook that addressed his adolescent strengths and weaknesses, and what he needed to develop in his own "game." Its validity as a playbook ultimately lay in whether it worked—did Arnold Palmer discover his craft, his excellence, himself?

This example involves a man, but it could just as easily involve a woman. The soccer player Mia Hamm comes to mind immediately as a woman who, during adolescence, developed her own playbook of success, with the help of mentors and other social connections.

Every adolescent is trying to develop a playbook right now, in your classroom—and playbooks don't always relate to athletics. Every adolescent is seeking a direction and purpose in life—and needs help from teachers and friends to find it. Every adolescent wants a playbook that provides wisdom (from within and without) and accepts innovation and novelty. Every teacher has the power to help his or her students develop their individual playbook. This book of relevance and purpose and novelty in learning can help organize education for an adolescent around strengths and weaknesses; it can open up new ways of thinking and doing; and it is goal focused in clear, understandable ways for the child, even if the boy or girl one day throws it out and begins writing a new one.

Looking to Coaches' Playbooks for Models

Have you ever borrowed a coach's playbook? Coaches use them for team sports especially, most notably football and basketball. To accomplish the team's goal of winning games, the coach fills the playbook with a broad array of strategies—pass plays, getting the ball in the hands of a variety of receivers; running plays, going inside, outside, reverses; trick plays that no one expects. Coaches are constantly on the lookout for new plays. They watch other teams and their own players to try to develop new strategies for achieving their goal. Coaches even design special plays when they have a player with a specific skill that they think will benefit the team.

Begin thinking about playbooks by asking yourself questions about your classroom of kids:

Do I have a variety of strategies in place for learning, so that each child's style can find a good learning environment?

Do I help each adolescent adjust to his or her strengths and weaknesses?

Do I try something different and unique from time to time to see what happens?

Do I help students experience a sense of purpose and relevance in what I teach?

Do I help the neediest students develop a playbook and set goals?

Do I use colleagues as resources to make sure I am always expanding my personal playbook?

As a middle or high school teacher, you may not feel you have time in the day to be a "coach" for every single student; however, you will notice immediately the boys and girls in your classroom who will not succeed without your being a coach. You can provide a playbook and help the students develop one for themselves.

TRY THIS Begin a Playbook for Yourself and for Each Student

For and with each student, answer these questions:

1. What are this student's strengths as a learner?

2. What are his or her weaknesses as a learner?

3. What are his or her favorite activities, inside and outside class?

4. What do these favorite activities show about his or her strengths and weaknesses?

5. How does this student integrate peers into learning?

6. When do peers distract this student from learning?

7. Who are this student's mentors?

8. How would this student answer the question, "What do I want to do in life?"

9. How would he or she answer the question, "What is my purpose on this earth?"

It is sometimes interesting to fill in answers yourself and ask the adolescent boy or girl to do the same (in different locations), then come together to compare notes.

Now answer each of the questions for yourself as a teacher (changing the language, of course). See what your own playbook as a teacher might look like.

After you've answered the questions for both yourself and your student and talked together about the issues raised in the answers regarding the student, here are two other specific questions that have a great deal to do with these next chapters. Ask them with and for your student:

1. What kind or style of learner is this boy or girl? Specifically, is this adolescent more of a verbal-emotive learner or a spatial-mechanical learner?

2. How much and when do peers, mentors, coaches, parents, and other relationships affect this boy's or girl's ability to learn?

Answer these questions now, then answer them again after you've read this and the next chapter. You might find interesting resonances and new ideas.

Teaching to the Strengths of Boys and Girls: How the Playbook Can Work

Students will come to you with an array of natural strengths, abilities, and interests. Their elementary school experience may or may not have encouraged each of them to excel, to stretch, and to believe in themselves as learners. Puberty will be setting in and impacting their ability to "keep their heads in the game." Your job, especially in the middle school years, is often quite a challenge, and disorganization is one of your enemies. It can also be your students' enemy—if their homework is not, for instance, relevant to their personal playbook, they may think of it as extraneous, and not do it. If they get caught up in social groups and lose a sense of how a new friend fits their own playbook, they can become lost to learning.

If you work with your students to answer crucial questions regarding their strengths, weaknesses, and goals, you can begin to help them focus on a possible playbook approach—organization from the inside out. This playbook idea can work for you because it individualizes learning. In this chapter, we look at developing a playbook for learning that helps expand learning strategies beyond the traditional classroom; in the next chapter, we look at how to expand the idea of a playbook to include mentors and friends as learning partners. Both will enable you to add constantly to your playbook for a given boy or girl.

As you move through this material, we hope you'll meet with each boy and girl and talk about the playbook. For some students, the idea of a playbook won't be necessary—they can learn anywhere at any time! But for many, it can be a real boon. Parents can also become involved in creating the playbook. This book—or as one teacher calls it, "a student's book of life for this adolescent period," can include parents', teachers', and students', even grandparents' and friends' ideas of a particular adolescent's strengths, weaknesses, and goals.

Although we can certainly say that this idea of a playbook is helpful to both boys and girls, that does not negate the crucial role of gender. Boys are becoming men, and girls are becoming women. The playbook of each works best if it includes gender-specific strengths, weaknesses, and goals.

Here's an example. In one girl's playbook, her verbal strengths were clear—she learned well by reading, writing, listening, and speaking. She was not as strong athletically, and she didn't like such games as chess. She wanted, however, to go into medicine later in life. She, her teachers, and her parents got involved in some of the material you are about to work with, and they put together a playbook that included this student's receiving tutoring help in math and participating in chess club. Maybe she would not go into medicine—goals change—but certainly she couldn't move in that direction if she didn't improve her math skills. Her playbook set her up to pursue that assistance.

Another example: a fourteen-year-old boy wanted to write science fiction one day. He was strong in science, but not in writing. He was also doing badly in math—not turning in homework, bored, not learning; yet as a football player he understood his coach's very complex football playbook. His coach saw this boy's adolescence as being "like his hair—disheveled." Coach, parents, teachers, and this boy together developed a playbook by which he would get homework done, get help in the writing lab, and direct himself toward his goal.

Creating a Playbook

Let your students decide if they would like to make an actual playbook, and provide them with materials to do so if they choose. The girls may want to write in their book, use graphics, pictures from magazines, all variety of media to make the playbook come alive. Boys may be interested too, or they may carry their playbook around in their head, using their visual-spatial resources to picture it in their mind. Both are good ways to create a playbook; each student's choice is itself an expression of his or her strengths. Make sure the students know that the playbook is a personal item—they don't have to share it with anyone unless they choose to.

The metaphor of the playbook is ultimately a functional metaphor for goal setting. It can work for you and your most disorganized students because it forces the child and his or her community to focus on how the child's brain already learns well, what the child is weak in, and what parts of that combination keep the child from succeeding at reaching crucial goals.

Consider also the importance of developing a common set of terminology in a playbook. Teachers across a school very often do not share a common instructional language. For example, what we name the different forms of writing varies from source to source. Nevertheless, wherever and whenever possible, we must choose to keep our instructional language consistent. Personal narratives are frequently called "recounts." Nonfiction is often called "expository." For visual-spatial learners, this changing terminology can be particularly challenging. We recommend keeping the instructional language simple and straightforward; otherwise, it gets confusing fast—even for older students and adults. Developing a common instructional language that is used consistently throughout the school is even more important for your visual-spatial thinkers!

As you move through this metaphor of the playbook and your own process of developing one for each boy and girl, look immediately for ways to get help for each student. When adolescents are involved in planning and controlling their own future, their brains release feel-good neurotransmitters, such as serotonin, dopamine, and norepinephrine-adrenaline. They neurally "buy into" the process of learning in which you are hoping to engage them.

The concept of the playbook becomes a tool for understanding and directing students. As such, it will often, and relatively quickly, reveal learning style issues for certain boys and girls. One that quickly shows up involves the way a typical classroom is set up—as if for those students whose playbook is dominated by verbal learning strategies. Let's move now to expanding our teaching playbook beyond this way of teaching. A number of students will become better able to find direction, purpose, and learning strength through our expansion of teaching into their way of learning. This is going to be especially true of boys.

Consider the typical classroom environment: there's lecture and discussion, reading and writing, speaking and listening—a wonderfully rich tapestry of verbal exchange. Language dominates. Almost exclusively, language is the vehicle through which knowledge is presented, practiced, assimilated, and assessed in the classroom.

Fortunately, many of your students may have good language acumen. These are the students who have thrived and will continue to thrive in the typical school setting; however, there are many students whose strengths lie elsewhere. The "verbal playbook" may not work for them. Nearly one-half of your class may be hard-wired for greater strengths in the visual-spatial arena than in the verbal-emotive arena. These students might be adept at watching objects move through space, rotating objects in space in their mind's eye without a physical model, solving visual puzzles, and engaging in higher-level reasoning in the spatial domain. They might learn more easily and problem-solve more effectively when they are working on tasks requiring visual-spatial thinking because they have a greater number of cortical areas dedicated to visual-spatial processing. Oftentimes, five to ten of your male students and two or three of your female students might be advantaged in this area.

This is not to say that these same students cannot perform well verbally—many of them can and do. But many—especially males—may not. Let's suppose that you want your students to write a paper. In both your own and your students' playbook, "writing" may right now mean "using words." Ultimately, of course, it does—but must it begin that way? What if you change your playbook to better accommodate the strengths and weaknesses of your visual-spatial boys (and girls)? What if, for instance, you let students—should they need to—draw storyboards of what they are going to write about? For between seven and ten students, this may ultimately lead to better papers—more detailed, better outlined, richer in critical thinking. This little adaptation in the playbook can bring great results, as a number of the schools trained in gender differences have shown.

See how this approach might fit your classroom. Notice whether your male-brained students express less sensory detail in their writing than your female-brained students. Because females have more acute, detailed perception of sight, sound, and touch, and more neural connectivity between the "feeling" center of the brain and the "thinking" center of the brain, they often show greater skill in putting detail and feeling into words. Perhaps you might have listed "sensory detail" as a strength of certain girls when you began your playbook for them. If you've compared boys' and girls' writing before, you've probably noticed the difference in the number of words in their pieces, the difference in sentence complexity, and the difference in use of descriptive language.

Allow for and teach more visual-spatial prewriting, and you will see some (though not all) of this gap close. Furthermore, change your playbook to include letting your boys and girls read more of what they care about—and write about it—and the papers can get even better. Girls find heroes among women (not just male heroes from books written by men), and boys may find nonfiction assets—such as biographies of sports figures—with which they can identify more easily than "girl-type" books. These biographies often involve more visual-spatial information (especially if they are about any kind of sport) and better stimulate the language centers and interests of some boys.

Some kids can take the shortest route to being good at writing, and need no alteration in their playbook. They simply pick up the pencil, draft a plan, and start to write. More often, you will notice that this is the route chosen by girls in your class. Others need to take the scenic route, so to speak, and they need help in organizing and in getting to their purpose. They need to create images in their mind and pictures on paper. They need to organize ideas in space before organizing them in words. They need a different playbook.

These thoughts did not come in any verbal formulation. I rarely think in words at all. A thought comes, and I may try to express it in words afterward.

—Albert Einstein

Using Graphic Organizers (a Powerful Playbook)

Many teachers already use graphic organizers in their classroom, and research unequivocally supports their use. With an understanding of the male and female brain, we can develop a greater understanding of how and why the graphic organizer works to support organization, sensory detail, fluency, word choice, and other features of writing.

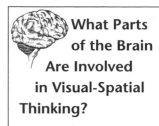

What Parts of the Brain Are Involved in Visual-Spatial Thinking?

Hippocampus: stores and processes spatial information. It acts as a *cognitive map*—a neural representation of the layout of the environment.

Right hemisphere: governs spatial thinking. Memory is stored in auditory, visual, and spatial modalities.

Corpus collosum: the neural highway that exchanges information between the right and left hemispheres of the brain.

Supramarginal gyrus: involved in spatial meaning; guides action—for example, coordinating how a person moves his or her hand toward a glass of water.

Thalamus: the brain's key sensory relay system.

Occipital lobes: used for visual input and visualizing. Specifically, it is responsible for color recognition, and it controls vision.

Parietal lobes: responsible for sensory sorting, spatial orientation, and visual perception.

A graphic organizer is a visual representation of knowledge. It is itself a playbook—a way to structure information and arrange it so that it visually represents the organization of one's ideas. Graphic organizers can be used to compare, contrast, sequence, and expand ideas. Once formulated, they can provide a record of one's thinking, a "book" for how to proceed with a project, or a review sheet for what has been learned. Following a lesson, the process of trying to capture the main concepts and transpose them into a graphic representation is a high-level synthesis task in itself. Using graphic organizers can be especially helpful in getting girls to use their visual-spatial resources—helping them move from the more abstract visuals to the more concrete verbals.

The following sections describe four main ways that graphic organizers organize and represent knowledge. If you don't use any other kind of play-book, at least make sure to help your most strongly visual-spatial students develop graphic organizers that include a combination of words, pictures, and symbols.

Hierarchical Organizers   This organizer includes a main concept and sub-concepts under it. For example, a class may be studying the main events leading up to revolution—the American or French, perhaps. Subconcepts would be written or symbolized in the organizer. Or perhaps your student is supposed to write a persuasive essay, such as why people should not smoke. The three subconcepts would be the three main reasons for not smoking, along with details to support the reasons. The visual structure of this graphic organizer matches the verbal structure of a five-paragraph essay.

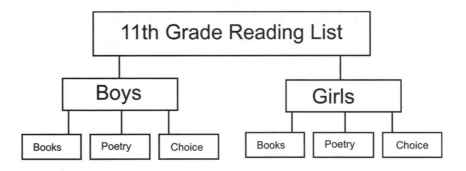

Conceptual Organizers   This organizer includes a central idea or category about which you want students to develop supporting facts, such as examples or characteristics. This is an excellent organizer for descriptive writing. For example, students might be describing a place that is special to them. They can use the concept map to record details derived from the five senses—what they see, hear, feel, smell, and taste. Venn diagrams aid in tasks requiring comparing and contrasting. Because these organizers do not impose a sequence of thoughts, they are good for brainstorming but not necessarily for creating the linear structure required for a report. They do not provide a "visual plan" for the organization of a piece of writing, and they can be overused. Consider having students use a conceptual organizer for brainstorming and one of the other organizers for creating a logical sequence of ideas.

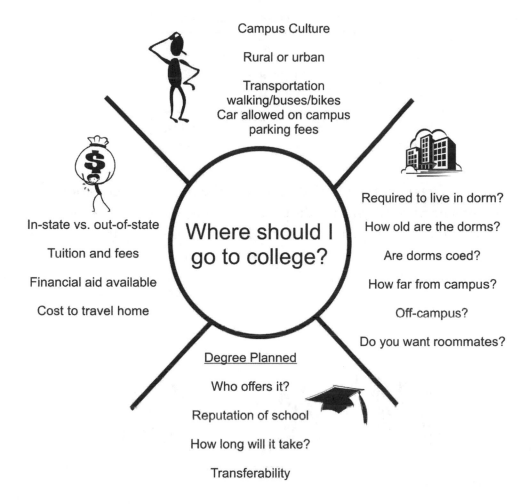

Campus Culture

Rural or urban

Transportation
walking/buses/bikes
Car allowed on campus
parking fees

Where should I go to college?

Required to live in dorm?

How old are the dorms?

Are dorms coed?

How far from campus?

Off-campus?

Do you want roommates?

In-state vs. out-of-state

Tuition and fees

Financial aid available

Cost to travel home

Degree Planned

Who offers it?

Reputation of school

How long will it take?

Transferability

Sequential Organizers   This organizer arranges events in a chronological order. It can be used for beginning-middle-end, cause-effect, chronology, or problem-solution. It can also be a storyboard, which works especially well for students who find comic books and graphic novels appealing. The sequential organizer can be used effectively for recounting historical events or telling a fictional or nonfictional story. The rising-action plotline can be especially helpful for students writing fiction. A plot is itself a form of playbook, and talking about it with students can help them see strengths, weaknesses, and purpose or goal. As the sequential time line of events helps students visualize how the problem in the story is established, climaxes, and then resolves, students can keep in mind that authors often start with the most exciting or climactic moment first to grab their reader's attention, so sequential organizers don't always work as designed.

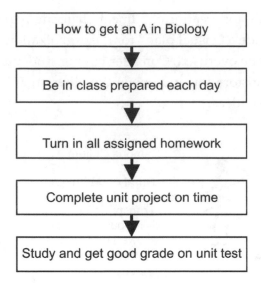

Cyclical Organizers   This kind of organizer represents a series of events comprising a process, such as the life cycle. It is a good organizer for showing how one step or event leads to another, and has some natural applications in science. It also works well for writing "circle stories"—stories that come back to where they started.

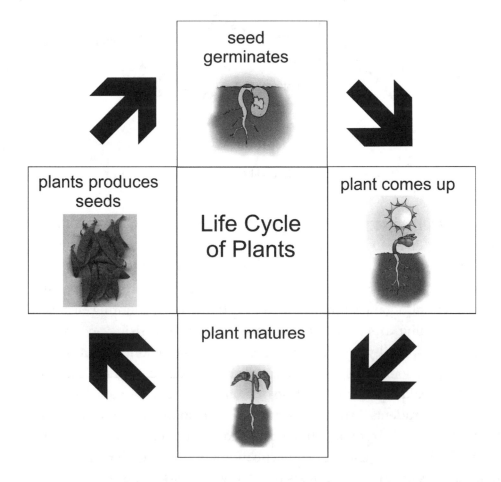

Utilizing More Drawing and Symbol Making

Students are never too old to pull out the colored pencils. Unfortunately, some of the best multisensory teaching strategies are left in the dust as students move into the higher grades. That need not be the case. Creating symbols and pictures to represent knowledge is a powerful way to reinforce students' understanding. It can be surprisingly difficult to convey meaning without the use of words, so the exercise in itself can become a high-level synthesis and meaning-making activity. The exercise allows your visual-spatial learners to shine and challenges your more verbal learners, often your highly verbal girls, to expand their own playbook—thinking and expressing differently than they are used to.

Here is a quick exercise you can use in class after new information is presented:

Have students close their eyes and review what they have just learned and then draw a picture or pictures to demonstrate visually what they know. Then have them turn and share their drawing and its meaning with a partner, after which you continue with the lesson. Be sure to note which students readily embrace this activity and which ones complain that it is too hard or cumbersome. Does a gender difference show up? It will reveal a lot about the learning styles of your students!

Picture-and-symbol exercises of this kind can also be used prior to teaching a lesson, as a way of assessing background knowledge. Post butcher paper on the wall and have students come up and sketch what they already know. When they are done, have them sit down and discuss the pictures and their meanings as a group. What do students already know about the topic? What new information do they want to know? Those ideas can be sketched as well.

If you use a word or concept wall (a wall to list vocabulary or big ideas) in your classroom, consider dressing up the list with students' illustrations. This also works well with any list of ideas, including a list of the classroom rules. Ed DaSilva, science teacher at the Saint Louis School in Honolulu, has his students illustrate the rules for use of the science lab by creating safety cartoons. He reports that this helps students remember the rules and take greater ownership of them. Here are two examples that his students shared with us.

Other teachers have students illustrate key vocabulary and then display it in the classroom as a great teaching and learning resource. The pairing of the words and the pictures supports both male and female learning styles in the classroom:

au stere-bleak; somber; grave

In-vec-tive $\frac{5}{5}$ PP

Invective

Definition: Invective = noun: Denunciatory or
abusive language; vituperation.

Sonia

Next time you look at student drawings, notice the detail that conveys thoughts about the characters, the setting, and the action. The drawings often also capture great sensory detail that can be transferred into the children's writing. Conference with students (or have them conference with each other) about their drawings just as you would conference with them

about their writing. Having students talk about their drawings (and the story they depict) activates the organizational centers in the frontal lobe and serves as an important step in helping students bridge from visual-spatial thinking to verbal production.

In expanding your teaching in this direction, you are, perhaps without being fully able to track it, affecting the playbook of many of your students. Many of these students will now feel they "fit" with learning, and will feel learning becoming more relevant to them—their purpose in life, their future success, their work possibilities. The "big concept" of the playbook can become immediately felt in this way.

Integrating Technology Education into Your Classroom

Technology is a motivating learning tool for many students, especially those who are already using it in their home or out-of-school playbook. As a visual medium, it is a primary communication tool for visual-spatial learners—especially your boys. And by focusing on technology, female students can benefit from additional visual-spatial exercises that can help develop skills and confidence in an area where they are underrepresented in the professional world.

Graphic organizers on the computer. Created for upper elementary through secondary students, Inspiration is a software program that provides an easy way to apply the proven principles of visual learning. Students build graphic organizers by combining pictures, text, and spoken words to represent thoughts and information. Students improve comprehension skills and better organize ideas for writing. Use Inspiration with interactive whiteboards to encourage whole-class collaboration in brainstorming, organization, and writing activities. Computerized graphic programs are very popular with boys, who tend to be comfortable with technology. Encouraging girls to use technology for prewriting tasks gets them using their less preferred spatial resources before relying on their more preferred verbal skills.

Drawing and painting on the computer. A good program for student-generated graphics is Adobe Photoshop. Without getting too technical, you can create graphics on a computer in two ways:

- *Drawing,* in a software application, means using tools that create "objects," such as squares, circles, lines, or text, that the program treats as discrete units. If you draw a square in Photoshop, for example, you can click anywhere on the square and move it around or resize it. It's an object, just like a typed letter *e* in a word processor.

- *Painting* functions, in contrast, don't create objects. If you look at an image on a computer screen, you'll see that it's made up of millions of tiny dots called pixels. You'll see the same thing in a simpler form if you look at the color comics in the Sunday newspaper—lots of dots (in four colors of ink) that form a picture. Unlike a drawing function, a paint function changes the color of individual pixels based on the tools you choose. In a photograph of a person's face, for example, the colors change gradually because of light, shadow, and complexion. You need a paint function to create this kind of effect.

Multimedia tools on the computer. PowerPoint is a well-known application for creating multimedia presentations. It allows students to present their knowledge in a slide-show format that is fairly simple and straightforward to use. Expand your classroom playbook, when you can, to include the use of this tool. PowerPoint has many features for advanced users and would provide a wonderful challenge (including the use of customized animation of graphics and effects) for your students who need additional challenge.

Students who are less comfortable standing in front of the class and giving a report can find it easier to make a technology-assisted presentation. While his or her classmates focus on the presentation, the presenter can feel a little less under the spotlight.

Digital stills and movies. Perhaps you've decided to have students do a documentary for their culminating project. Students can use digital technology to take still photos or movie footage. A photo editing program, such as Adobe Photoshop, will give students experience with an application that most professionals use. For digital movies, students can use an editing application such as iMovie or Toast.

Perhaps you worry about getting involved in technology projects because you aren't as familiar with them as you feel you need to be to assess your students' work. There are many resources available in your community to help. There may be other faculty, or even students in a computer club, who would love to tutor you in the programs you want to learn. And remember, every time we learn a new skill, we grow new neural connections no matter what our age!

Also remember that you can bring in volunteers from the local community—parents, college students, people from business—to work with your students. Make sure to find both male and female volunteers, especially women professionals in the technology field, who can share how they use technology in their work.

"I had this teacher who let us compare what we learned to The Terminator. He also let us make a homemade video about the unit."

—12th grade boy

"I want to do something creative, colorful, and visual, such as a PowerPoint or a poster. I think creating something based on the material ensures that you really understand it."

—12th grade girl

"We need more visual learning skills and less lectures. I like stuff that I can feel and visualize."

—8th grade boy

Using More Manipulatives and Physical Models

"Science," states high school teacher Kristin Donley, "is just chock full of hands-on opportunities due to the nature of the subject." Kristin recently had students build three-dimensional DNA molecules, and the sky was the limit. One group of students took pictures of themselves with various facial expressions and used them to make the base pairs in the DNA molecule. Another student knitted a scarf based on the cytochrome C protein code. Kristin also works with team teacher Tony Tolbert to do interclass projects. Tony's core biology class is preparing skits to teach AP biology students about pathogens, and Kristen's AP students are preparing a musical to teach Tony's students about DNA replication and how proteins are made. They plan to film their performances and perform for friends and family in the auditorium.

What's exciting about what these students are doing is twofold. First, students are allowed to learn and be assessed in ways that match their learning styles, with options that allow all students to shine—including the visual-spatial learners, especially the males. Second, students are given a say in the projects they do. This can be a powerful motivator for adolescents, and it especially keys into young men's need to find relevance in what they are doing.

Wisdom of Practice: Teachers in Action

High school teacher Tracy Brennan will often ask her students to pick a favorite passage from the literature, such as *Heart of Darkness* or Dante's *Inferno,* and have them draw a scene from the text. She looks for symbolic elements and understanding of the text other than what would go into a list of answers to written questions or an essay. Sometimes the students

> **?**
>
> ### DID YOU KNOW? A New Playbook Helps Girls
>
> There is urgency around the use of visual-spatial learning strategies for many middle and high school teachers, as boys are statistically more likely to have lower grades and higher dropout rates than girls. The traditional verbal classroom is often not a fit for many of their brains.
>
> Visual-spatial strategies—and the expansion of our teaching playbook to include them more fully—are also helpful for girls. Brain research over the last two decades has shown that manipulatives and physical models have special significance for the thinking and learning of females. Male students are often more comfortable learning astronomy, physics, and other highly abstract, highly symbolic sciences. Often girls need more support in thinking visually and spatially. They often need more practice with the concepts through the use of hands-on materials that they can touch, rotate, and manipulate.

come up with ideas that she had never thought of before, and often the students who have trouble expressing themselves in written form will do amazing artwork while demonstrating a true understanding of the text.

Before reading *To Kill a Mockingbird*, teacher Ginny Vidulich preteaches all the vocabulary by having students illustrate the words and their meanings in a comic book style. Students have to figure out how to represent their word visually, they must use color, and their illustrations often incorporate a memorable bit of adolescent humor. Students share their word illustrations and, through the sharing process, the vocabulary concepts are reviewed and reinforced. This way, students begin reading the novel with greater confidence and success.

Seventh-grade science teacher Gregg Cruger teaches a unit on genetic cloning and has students demonstrate their understanding through a variety of visual-spatial tasks. Students are able to pick from a menu of project items, including designing a poster, a bumper sticker, or a CD album cover. To culminate another unit of study on plant and animal cells, Gregg has students create a three-dimensional cell out of any materials they want. One student recently baked a half-sphere cake and used a variety of candies to represent the different parts of the cell.

Ben Boyer's botany class incorporates many visual-spatial learning and assessment activities. For example, students can choose to visit the local Butterfly Pavilion and then draw or photograph five different butterflies. Students then mount the photos or drawings along with the scientific and common name of each butterfly. An alternative is to design a butterfly garden for their backyard. They complete a colored sketch of the garden and a list of at least fifteen plants used, including the plant's scientific and common name, the bloom season, and the bloom color. After teaching students the importance of plants to humans, Ben offers a variety of follow-up activities that include making a coloring book that shows chloroplast structure and function, building a composting bin for their home, and completing an Internet scavenger hunt.

Pam Brenner's seventh graders put their knowledge of ratios and proportions to work by building a miniature golf course hole to scale. With a list of specifications in hand, students decide on a measurement scale and then create a model with any materials they choose. Students have fun working hands-on to creatively design their hole with obstacles, features, and a theme of their choosing. All the mathematical calculations are recorded and turned in with their completed scale model. When all the projects come in on the due date, students have some time to actually "play" each other's holes.

Practical Ideas for Your Classroom

Throughout this chapter, you have read about a number of different activity ideas for increasing the visual-spatial learning opportunities in your classroom. Here are some suggestions on how to get started with some of these activities in your own classroom immediately.

Graphic Organizer Race   Put students in teams and give them five minutes to draw on chart paper as many types of graphic organizers as they can think of. When the time is up, check to see how many each group came up with. Combine everyone's ideas to create a longer master list of graphic organizers. Try different team configurations—all girls, all boys, mixed. Are the results any different?

Classifying Organizers   Have students work with a list of graphic organizers (either developed in a Graphic Organizer Race or provided to them) to classify the organizers as cyclical, sequential, hierarchical, or chronological. Have them explain why they classified them as they did and how some organizers might fit in more than one category.

Finding the Purpose   Have students match different purposes of writing to different graphic organizers. Have them think about which organizers work the best, which are adequate, and which are not recommended for each of the purposes.

Wall Displays   Have students create exemplars of graphic organizers on chart paper to be displayed on the classroom walls for ongoing reference.

Comics and Graphic Novels   During free-choice writing, occasionally allow your students to select these genres. They can be part of a menu of options so that you can control how often students write in this form while still offering students choice. Students can also use these genres to convey their knowledge of the content in any subject area.

Classroom Rules   Have students illustrate "Dos and Don'ts" to spruce up your list of classroom rules. They will not only enjoy drawing but also find it humorous and get a laugh from their peers.

Drawing to Summarize   Have students create a four-panel coat of arms to depict what they've just learned, sketch a book cover that captures the main idea or problem, or draw a bird's-eye view of the setting of the event or story.

Word Walls and Big Ideas   Challenge your students to use pictures (and no words) to convey the meaning of key vocabulary, main ideas, and concepts. Students can also complete a K-W-L chart (what they *know,* what they *want* to know, and what they *learn*) with pictures and symbols only.

Pictographs   Challenge students to illustrate a poem, story, or section of their textbook using an original system of symbols and pictures, such as pictographs.

♎ ⤴ ♎ ◗ 🖼 🗂 🐚 ⌘

Set Design   Get students involved with building and designing sets for a classroom or school play. Have them calculate the cost of supplies, measure the materials, and construct the sets. This is a great way to integrate math and science skills.

Technology   Be sure to take advantage of the wonderful visual-spatial learning activities that various technology media offer.

WRAPPING UP THE MAIN POINTS

- Each teacher and each student benefits from developing a playbook of what he or she is doing as a teacher or a learner

- Playbooks can be developed with the help of parents, members of the extended family, mentors, and friends.

- Playbooks help students and their support systems focus on strengths, weaknesses, and goals.

- The concept of the playbook includes expanding teaching beyond traditional methods and approaches to include a wider variety of "plays" that build on kids' strengths and interests.

- Specifically, a lot of students, including many boys, discover purpose, relevance, goals, and their own strengths by learning in more visual-spatial ways.

- Girls benefit from expanding their own gender playbook beyond the verbal modality.

From graphic organizers to computer-generated images, greater use of technology can benefit both boys and girls.

Building Learning Teams of Boys and Girls

Promoting Positive Social Development

I get by with a little help from my friends.

—John Lennon

A COACH of under-14 soccer recently told us, "When I coach girls, I make sure they have time to bond with one another—talk, connect verbally—for a few minutes before we begin our drills and activities. I learned the hard way that I need a somewhat different social plan for girls than boys." This coach, a man in his forties who had coached boys for twenty years, came to a training on how boys and girls learn differently and ended up teaching everyone in the room a great deal about adapting the "social playbook" to fit boys and girls.

Your middle school or high school is a place your students come not only to learn but to socialize. As you already know, their relationships are a powerful and motivating influence in their education, for both boys and girls. In their future adulthood, their work and social lives will be interconnected constantly—as right now, instruction and relationship are completely intertwined.

In Chapter Three, we looked at the metaphor of the playbook, and challenged you and your students to adapt personal playbooks toward purpose and relevance, and instructional playbooks toward an underused way of learning. In this chapter, we'd like to help you focus on and, when necessary, even adapt your playbook to address the social side of your teaching—the give-and-take, collaboration, and cooperation—that perhaps you haven't looked at before, especially in terms of specific adolescent boys and girls.

In our action research, middle and high schools have reported reductions in discipline referrals resulting from this focus; in some cases, teachers and principals have observed positive changes in students' academic performance as well.

The Importance of Social Relationships to the Education of Adolescent Boys and Girls

In collaboration with one another, students can solve problems, present and consider differing points of view, review prior knowledge, develop new strategies, share ideas, "talk out loud" as they work through issues, brainstorm, debate, organize their thinking, develop empathy, shift points of view, hone questioning skills, and expand their understanding of the world. Have you noticed some students becoming committed to a task through group interaction? Some students put in more effort because of the group. Sometimes a group creates immediate accountability.

Some students start out being pretty ineffective in groups, and have to learn how to work better in them. As the student's ability to relate increases, often so too does his or her ability to learn. As Daniel Goleman has pointed out in *Emotional Intelligence*, essential learning skills linked to self-awareness, mood management, motivation, empathy, and interpersonal relations can be learned, and often are well learned by adolescents in their classrooms. Interestingly, teenagers are often *not* adept readers of social signals, even though many teenagers seem to do nothing but socialize. These skills need to be systematically taught and learned. Group interaction can help.

As you might suspect, there are fascinating differences between males and females in groups. The brain is biologically programmed to focus first on information that has strong emotional content. Because their female brain is more attuned to emotive processing, girls may, on average, want to socialize, verbally, a great deal; through this strategy, in group or partner work, they may be using social interaction in the classroom to complete instructional tasks more successfully.

Boys will certainly talk as well while completing tasks—with more competitive talk—and often we find that their social interactions during instruction are useful for keeping the male brain out of a boredom or rest state, thus enhancing focus and shared purpose in their action.

When we work with parents as part of school training programs, some parents share concern about their children being "forced" to work on group projects in general, and gender-specific groups in particular. They might say, "My kid's grade depends on other kids doing their work, and that's not fair," or "Kids have to socialize with the other gender in real life; why separate them in adolescence?"

When parents hear some of the answers teachers and trainers have to share, they often feel more comfortable. Group work and collaborative learning have been shown to help in achievement, and gender-specific groups have been shown to help both with achievement and test scores and with discipline referrals. Coed groups are good; single-gender groups

TRY THIS Working in Gender-Specific Groups

Over the last decade, we have helped many middle and high school teachers innovate toward working with single-sex groups. Some teachers have found this a useful addition to their playbook. It grows from our looking, with teachers, at gender-based behavioral differences in males and females in groups.

Boys often quite naturally become more highly engaged in learning when there is an edge of competition to a project, and they tend to inject competition into a process. In an effort to motivate boys in healthy ways, teachers have tried male-only groups. The results are often stunning. We think part of what's happening for boys in these groups is that competition plays a crucial role in stimulating the reward centers in the brain.

Girls will tend to do more overall processing during group work than boys. They tend to be more concerned about seeing that everyone is included and to spend more time picking a leader. They will also take in more opinions during a task—working less from an "alpha" orientation and more from one of consensus. Boys often find aspects of this style boring. They might work for girls but not for boys, in the same way that girls often find excessive male competition silly.

Gender-specific groups allow more clear instruction and project time than a coed group might. In working on a project with members only of their own gender, girls and boys avoid the adolescent hormone-charged "mating behaviors" that can sometimes hamper them (girls dumbing themselves down to feed male egos, males posturing to compete for females).

The following student comments show the gamut of possibilities in social groupings. Students are anecdotal observers, but they are often very wise and concise.

"Sometimes in mixed groups, kids don't concentrate as well as boy only or girl only groups because they are busy trying to impress the opposite gender." (7th grade girl)

"Activities that allow for teamwork or competition make school a more interesting environment. I like teaming with both boys and girls, but it's a different experience each way!" (10th grade boy)

"When we do group work, I like girl-only groups, because we get more done than when we're with boys." (8th grade girl)

"I think all-boy groups work the best because boys know how boys work and what they are like which makes it easier to cooperate." (8th grade boy)

are good. Neither is superior; both are useful in the social-action playbooks that teachers, schools, parents, and students develop.

In our work with schools, we have come to believe that gender-specific group work is very helpful to girls who enter high-tech or high-stress professions. Women are often needed to mentor other women in these professions. Men need to do their part, but many of the businesses with which our corporate division has worked have found that female mentoring and female peer support systems are important for retention and advancement of women. As we help schools use single-gender groupings in math, science, language arts, and other classes, we believe we are helping girls learn to mentor each other in ways that will resonate for them as women in more traditionally male fields.

To see the logic of this, a teacher or school often must shift away from the widely held idea that the best way to train boys and girls is to "socialize" them all the time. Sometimes teachers need to add single-gender groupings to the playbook and see, after perhaps a month, just what happens. As a high school science teacher recently put it, "I don't like experts imposing an idea on me, so I resisted single-gender groupings. Now that I've tested it out myself, I'm sold on it. Both the boys and the girls learn more on specific projects, in my opinion. I wouldn't do it all the time—but for my class, it definitely works when it works."

Talent wins games, but teamwork and intelligence wins championships.
—Michael Jordan

Teamwork is the ability to work together toward a common vision. It is the fuel that allows common people to attain uncommon results.
—Andrew Carnegie

Which Parts of the Brain Contribute to Social Functioning?

Group work in general requires a complex exchange of information between the outside world and the brain. The brain engages all its lobes and other critical areas to take in information, access prior experience, process emotion, formulate language, and plan responses. Each of these areas of the brain are stimulated, which is one reason social functioning during instruction is so helpful to content learning; adding certain projects that are single gender adds novelty and variety to this brain functioning.

Frontal lobe: organizes and arranges information; coordinates planning, problem solving, judgment, the production of language, and the focusing of attention

Parietal lobe: processes sensory data and plays a part in language

Occipital lobe: processes visual input

Temporal lobe: responsible for hearing, senses, language, learning, and memory

Limbic system: comprises a number of connected structures involved in emotional response, including the hypothalamus, amygdala, thalamus, fornix, hippocampus, and cingulate gyrus

Broca's area: responsible for oral language production

Wernicke's area: responsible for language comprehension

Testosterone: surges through the male system more than once during childhood and in great amounts during puberty

Oxytocin: involved in social recognition and bonding

Adapting Your Social Interactions Playbook

Looking at social interactions in general, and touching on gender-specific group work, we've been looking at social interactions and social teams as learning vehicles. Perhaps you already utilize learning teams, and perhaps you've done team building with your class. If you have not done any, or have only done a little, we hope you'll expand your use of these approaches, and we'll show you ways to do it. You might well rescue certain boys and girls from struggling, and even from failure, by making learning more of a team approach.

Team Building

To create a successful team atmosphere in your classroom, it is important to begin with an awareness of the characteristics of a team and the benefits of teamwork. You can work with your students first to see what they already know about teams and teamwork before supplementing their thinking with the research. Have them brainstorm the characteristics of a team and the benefits of working together. Ask questions with them:

Are there frustrations related to working in a group?

What class rules or norms can we develop to minimize problems and frustrations?

Once students establish norms that they can all agree to, you and the students can refer to physical education teacher Zack Dee's tips on team-building (www.sonoma.edu/kinesiology/ppep/experts/team.htm) to see if they overlooked anything. Ask your students to think about whether they as individuals and as a class have these characteristics in their playbooks.

Tip 1: Characteristics of a Team

- All team members need to be aware of a sense of unity.

- Each member must have a chance to contribute and to learn from and work with others.

- The members must have the ability to act together toward a common goal.

- If the first three conditions aren't being met, the group needs to process and communicate until they are.

Tip 2: Benefits of Team Building

- *Perseverance.* It is important for students to understand that success doesn't always come easily. Failure only means that they need to try again or to rethink strategies.

- *Rules.* In team building there must be clearly stated rules. Whether they are for a game or for expected behaviors, rules must be set up to promote respect, responsibility, and safety, but at the same time they must be open enough to allow for student creativity, exploration, and experimentation. The consequences for failure to follow the rules should also be clear.

- *Social development.* It is important to remember in team building that the main objective is not necessarily to solve a specific challenge but to work effectively together as a group to try to complete the task at hand.

Ensuring That Girls Have a Voice

Especially in adolescence, some girls' voices can be drowned out in the often cacophonous and larger-than-life presence of more aggressive boys and girls. More so than boys, girls tend to focus on themselves and manipulate social networks through inclusion and exclusion. Girls also have a greater incidence of depression, eating disorders, and marked drops in self-esteem as they enter adolescence. They tend to care more about their appearance than do boys, and they more regularly subvert their own needs to meet the needs of other people.

In mixed-gender groups and classrooms, we need to be cognizant of the risk factors that crop up for adolescent girls. You may see girls becoming markedly less assertive in the company of boys, expressing a decreased level of enthusiasm for academics, or regularly deferring to male counterparts in activities involving math, science, or technology.

There are a few ways that you can help address this problem. Make sure that you call on girls as frequently as you call on boys. Make sure that boys do not handle or manipulate the materials or commandeer the computer to the exclusion of the girls during a group project. It can also help to establish group norms for classroom discussions so that students don't "step on each other's words." Structured discussion protocols are especially useful in making sure that every student can get his or her voice into the conversation and that all students develop good listening skills. For some activities, you may even choose to create single-sex groups, especially if the girls are not exercising the leadership skills you'd like when they're grouped with boys.

Wisdom of Practice: Teachers Doing the Work

Tracy Brennan's language arts students do a lot of interacting within the classroom setting. The class holds a "Socratic seminar" on every work that they read so that the students have a chance to interact and ask each other questions about the literature. Tracy told us,

I try to listen to the seminar, but not lead it, so that they can practice their skills in leadership and conversation. I would say that most of the boys are more involved in class when we are doing a Socratic seminar or when they get to participate in an active way, as in performing a scene from drama or creating a scenario from a novel. They seem to take the information in more readily when they get involved in some sort of physical way. Even changing the classroom configuration from straight rows of desks to a circle seems to get them more interested in learning and discussion of the literature. Another way to get them invested is to do group work on a large sheet of butcher paper in the hallway so they get to move around, change venues, get fresh air, and still focus on the work at hand.

The group work playbook that Tracy and her class have developed ensures that everyone in the group has a chance to speak and offer answers. Tracy's classes include small-group discussions during which students work collaboratively to answer questions about the literature and then turn in one set of answers. "They get very skillful at sharing information with one another and helping each other learn the material."

Science teacher Ben Boyer provides, within a menu of learning activities, the opportunity for his students to interact with the content in the social setting of a book club. Students select an approved book, such as *Ecotopia* or *Botany of Desire.* After reading it, they meet outside of school at an agreed-on location. The gathering is relaxed yet focused. Ben prompts the discussion if needed, but it is primarily facilitated by the students themselves. "I love hearing what kids have to say about the book, their lives and how the book relates to them," Ben says.

Practical Strategies for Your Classroom

The following is a list of team-building games and cooperative learning activities designed to help students get to know one another, increase communication and collaboration, improve classroom climate, and enhance student learning. Each one can be done in coed or gender-specific groups. As you institute them, you might enjoy keeping a journal of how boys and girls react differently. Some differences will be subtle but nevertheless very helpful in your constant efforts to ensure successful group work.

By the way, in addition to creating opportunities for social interaction, these activities make great brain breaks, as discussed in Chapter Two.

Meet Three People   Have students stand and shake hands with three people who . . . are wearing black, were born in the same state, have traveled outside the country, have an older sibling, were born in the same month, and so on. Note: Do you see any conscious (or unconscious) gender division as the groups form?

Musical Groups   Play some energizing music. Have students move around the classroom. When the music stops, have them take a seat at the nearest table group. This is a fun way to mix up your students so as to get them working with a different group from time to time.

Telling Yarns   Each student receives a piece of yarn. You can "assign" them a length or let them choose. One by one, the students tell a story about themselves while wrapping their piece of yarn around their finger. They keep talking until the yarn has been wrapped all the way around one finger. Note: If you let the students choose their own length of yarn, do you notice any difference between the boys and the girls in terms of the length of the pieces?

To Tell the Truth   Put students in small groups. Have each person write two true things about himself or herself and one untrue thing on an index card. Mix up the cards. Students take turns guessing which of the three items are true about their peers. Have them discuss how they tried to determine which was which.

String Geometry   Give each group of six to eight students a piece of string that is fifteen feet long. Have the groups make a series of different geometrical shapes, such as a triangle, octagon, or trapezoid. All members have to be holding on to the yarn. Make the activity more challenging by not allowing students to talk or by having them make the shapes with their eyes closed.

We're Different, We're Alike   Have students pair up. Give each pair a sheet of paper with a large Venn diagram on it. Have them discuss the ways that they are alike and different and then draw or write on the diagram to illustrate their conclusions. Share with the class.

Part of a Group   Give each student five small pieces of paper (each approximately two inches square). Have them think of five different groups they belong to—for example, a sports team, a scout troop, a reading group, a family, and so on. Have them illustrate each group with a symbol, one per square of paper. For the reading group, for example, the student may choose to draw a book. Take all the students' squares and arrange them on a large sheet of paper to show how many different groups there are and how many students belong to each kind of group. This activity may open up a discussion about cliques and other problems of social exclusiveness at school. It can also open discussion about gender differences in students' choices. This is a good conversation for young adults to have!

Classroom Quilt   Give each student two pieces of paper: a white five-by-five-inch square and a colored six-by-six-inch square. Have each child illustrate on the white paper something that is important to or about him or her. Mat it on the colored paper and then mount all the matted squares on a piece of butcher paper together to form a "quilt" that depicts the classroom community. Display it in the classroom to symbolize that every student is a part of the fabric of the classroom.

Teamwork in Action   Have students get into small groups of three to five students. Have them talk about situations in which they recently observed people working as a team (for example, at the grocery store, on the playground, at a sporting event). Have them describe what they observed. Discuss as a whole class and make note of the words used to describe how people interacted in these situations—"helping each other," "working together," "cooperating," and so on. Together, develop a definition of teamwork that can be displayed in the classroom.

Build It   Put students into groups of two or three. Give each group an equal number of straws or coffee stirrers and an equal length of masking tape. Give them a set amount of time in which to build the tallest freestanding structure they can. Note: pay attention to the processing differences if you divide the groups by gender.

Build It II   This time, put students in larger groups of six to eight students. Give each group four boxes, a roll of masking tape, a pair of scissors, a ruler, and a pencil or pen. Instruct the teams to build a chair (or other functional item of your or their choosing) using the supplies they've been given. When time is up, have the teams share their planning, decision-making, and building processes. "Try out" each other's creations.

Detective   Before you begin, choose two or three students to be detectives. Their task will be to find the leader of the "group." Have them hide their eyes while you silently indicate who among the remaining group is to be the leader. Have the entire group stand in a circle. The leader actually leads the group by making movements; the group conceals the leader by copying him or her. The detectives attempt to find the first one who changes the movement. The leader needs to change actions at least every ten seconds.

———————

Remember that virtually any classroom activity that can be done independently can be modified to be done in a cooperative group!

WRAPPING UP THE MAIN POINTS

- Intentionally planning how to utilize social interaction and group work in learning is an important way to expand our playbook.

- Both student achievement and discipline improve when social interactions are integrated into learning.

- Emotional intelligence is important to cognitive intelligence—group work and learning teams can increase this intelligence.

- Boys and girls experience social interactions in different ways.

- Gender-specific groups can be effective learning tools.

- Team building is simple and effective.

- Girls' voices can become lost in large groups—specific strategies can help girls succeed.

Letting Them Lead

The Power of Choice on the Developing Adolescent Brain

My mother's menu consisted of two choices: Take it or leave it.

—Buddy Hackett

IN today's world, adolescents are bombarded with choices, at least in the consumer world of what to wear, what to eat, what movies to see, and what music to listen to.

At the same time, much of an adolescent's learning life is often prescribed for them. High schools increasingly dictate what classes students must take. Electives that might look appealing in a student handbook are often unavailable due to the number of courses now required for graduation. Healthy choices, such as daily physical education classes, are rarely required anymore in an effort to make room for more academic courses. Classes that can lead to lifelong positive pursuits for the developing adolescent brain—band, choir, and art, for example—are becoming increasingly rare. Simultaneously, schools may offer as many as a hundred extracurricular activities from which students can choose, including sports programs, service and social clubs, volunteer opportunities, and the like—which to choose? Those activities along with hours of homework, part-time jobs, and family responsibilities can overwhelm and stress adolescents.

Meanwhile, the adolescent brain is developing its ability to make choices. Much of that brain's successful future in the world will depend not only on how it learns positive choice making but also on how the adults around the adolescent help his or her brain do that learning. This is a risk-taking brain—a lot of choice making is experiential, primal, sudden. The frontal cortex, where mature thinking takes place, where the brakes get put on so as to allow a person to stop, think, and consider consequences, isn't working at adult capacity. Adolescents will make a lot of

"I appreciate the non-traditional approach and being able to choose things that excite me. I do better and get better grades."

— 11th grade boy

"When I try to balance my school life and real life, I have to make choices. It's good for me."

— 10th grade girl

"For me, the big choices come from extracurricular activities, which I do not want to give up, and doing homework as soon as it's assigned."

— 10th grade girl

"Grades cause a lot of stress. There is so much competition between students that gets in the way of enjoying learning. I wish we could choose more of what we learn."

— 12th grade girl

"The most stressful aspect of teenage life is having the time-management skills needed to balance school, family and extra-curriculars. I have a job and play hockey on a competitive travel team so I typically don't get home and start homework until 7pm or later on weeknights."

— 12th grade boy

"Being a teenager sucks and always will. Relationships, not enough choices, too many choices, colleges, money problems, general ugliness in the world. No offense."

— 12th grade boy

choices that they don't think through completely. They will be encouraged by the group mentality of their peers—whose frontal cortices are also still maturing—to take ill-advised risks. When things go wrong, we will look at them and wonder, "What could they have been thinking?!" The answer is, of course, that they weren't thinking. They were making choices on impulse, driven by their need for novelty and excitement and their belief that they are in control.

Choice making is complex for adolescents and deeply affects their ability to learn. In this chapter, we will not solve all the issues of adolescent impulsivity, need, and drive—but we can look at choice making and learning, and very practically bring to the foreground an aspect of adolescent development about which we, as teachers, have a lot of choice.

Understanding How Choice Promotes Learning

Children are often criticized for "not paying attention." There is no such thing as not paying attention; the brain is always paying attention to something.

—Patricia Wolfe, *Brain Matters*

As children become adolescents, they increasingly want and need to be more independent and self-directed. In fact, allowing students to engage in new experiences and to make their own choices stimulates neurons that link emotional centers to other parts of the brain, causing the release of dopamine and resulting in feelings of pleasure. In addition, offering students choices engages the attention center of the brain and ensures that they have a personal interest in the topic. When learners feel that their choices are an important part of the learning process, their interest and accountability go up, and content retention increases drastically. For both boys and girls, this fills important neurological and emotional, as well as academic, needs.

Neurologically speaking, attention is a process of selecting the most relevant information from an overwhelming mass of sensory input around us. Focusing one's attention on something one can't figure out or doesn't understand not only becomes boring but is practically impossible! The secret to engaging students lies in understanding what it is that gets and keeps their attention.

Knowing that *making choices* and *responding to novelty* are part of the basic wiring of your students' developing adolescent brains, you can put together a plan of action that engages adolescent students and makes their learning experiences powerful.

What Parts of the Brain Are Responsible for Attention and Choice Making?

Reticular activating system: filters all incoming stimuli and makes the decision about what should be attended to or ignored. It acts like a sieve; some research indicates that 99 percent of all incoming sensory information is allowed to "pass through the sieve" because it is perceived to be irrelevant.

Limbic system: a group of interconnected deep-brain structures involved in a number of functions, including emotion, motivation, and behavior. The more emotion laden the stimulus, the better the chance of its attracting attention. Although girls tend to process more information through their limbic system to their cerebral cortex than boys, during adolescence both boys and girls have an overactive limbic system.

Left frontal lobe: exercises conscious control over one's thoughts to allow for focusing of attention, prioritizing, and problem solving. This area tends to mature faster in the female brain than in the male brain.

Amygdala: takes in converging sensory inputs to inform a person of potential dangers in the environment; also helps us notice and attend to novelty—novelty is an innate attention getter! The amygdala tends to be larger in the male brain, which can result in boys' being quick to become angry or aggressive.

Wisdom of Practice: What Teachers Are Doing

Sometimes you may feel that you can't offer students a great deal of choice because of the demands of a bloated curriculum and the pressure of testing. The examples in this section show how you needn't feel trapped in a choice-versus-curriculum "either-or" dichotomy.

Rachel Laufer and gifted education teachers in Harrison School District 2 have provided this example of a "novel choice board" students can use to select a culminating project. This innovative approach can incorporate a wide range of interests and appeal to the learning styles of both boys and girls in unique ways.

One way to incorporate choice in the semester-long teaching plan is to create study agreements with students. Science teachers at Boulder High School structure the semester around a set of required activities (70 percent of the grade) and several optional activities (30 percent of the grade). Required activities respond to both male and female learning styles and incorporate reading, hands-on lab work, an art project, in-class notes, completion of a study guide, and response to film questions. The following optional activities are offered in a botany class:

- Read and respond to journal articles.
- Review a Web site and write a one-page summary.
- Create a coloring book of specific content.
- Do an oral class presentation.

- Take a field trip and respond to questions.
- Conduct an Internet search and provide a write-up.
- Take gardening tools to the hardware store to be sharpened.
- Rub linseed oil on all wooden tool handles at home.
- Sample tea and concoct an original blend.
- Watch a PBS show and provide a one-page summary.
- Write a haiku poem and create original artwork about the concepts.
- Wrap the tree trunks of deciduous trees.
- Rake leaves and take them to the leaf drop-off site.
- Rake, bag, and recycle an elderly neighbor's leaves.
- Photo-document the tree-planting process and create a display.
- Create a collage of photos and text.
- Build a composting bin and review four related articles.
- Measure ten trees on the school campus and report results.
- Design a Feng Shui garden.
- Grow your own sprouts.

Novel Choice Activities

1. Make a collage that compares and contrasts the physical and personality traits between you and a character in the book. Make sure to describe the similarities and differences between you and the character.	2. Write a bio-poem about yourself and another main character in the book so that your readers see how similar or different you are from the character. Be sure to include the most important traits in each poem.	3. Write a recipe or set of directions for how you would solve a problem and another for how a main character in the book would solve a problem. Your list should help us know you and the character.
4. Choose a problem in your novel or short story and make a greeting card that illustrates the cause of the problem on the front cover and the effect it had on the character on the inside.	5. Choose at least ten items of fact and opinion from your story or novel and use a Venn diagram to show your findings. Why are some of the events both fact and fiction?	6. Take a situation from a novel and make a pro and con sheet illustrating the choices that the characters had. What choice did the character actually make? Do you think that this was the right choice?
7. Find out about famous people in history or current events whose experiences and lives reflect the essential themes of the novel. Make a poster describing the similarities.	8. Research a town that you feel is equivalent to the one in which your novel is set. Use maps, sketches, and population and other demographics to help you make comparisons and contrasts.	9. Authors have a wide variety of reasons that they write books and stories. Pretend that you are the author of the novel or story and write a letter to the editor explaining why he or she should purchase your piece of work.

Novel Analysis

Directions:

- Select a book that you have already read or are currently finishing.
- Read the book carefully.
- When you are finished, choose one activity from each column that appeals to you.
- If you have an idea of your own that is not on the chart, check with your teacher for permission to try it.
- Proofread and edit your work. Turn in your work for credit.

Character Analysis	*Plot Analysis*	*Setting Analysis*	*Novel Response*
1. Choose two main characters in the novel you are reading. Using a Venn diagram, compare and contrast the personality traits of those two characters.	2. Describe the problem or conflict existing for the main character in the book. Tell how the conflict was or was not resolved.	3. Research and write a two-page report on the geographical setting of your story. Include an explanation as to why this setting was important to the effect of the story.	4. Find a song or a poem that relates to the theme of your book. Explain the similarities and differences using quotes from the book and the song on a poster.
5. Choose one character in your book to interview. Create ten questions that you would like to ask your character. Pretend that you are the character and answer the questions.	6. Compare and contrast the conflict of your book with another book that you have read before. Compare your similarities and differences on a poster of the two books.	7. After reading a book of history or historical fiction, make an illustrated time line showing events of the story and draw a map showing the locations where the story took place.	8. Make models of three objects that were important in the book you read. On an index card attached to each model, tell why that object was important in the book.
9. Plan a party for at least four of the characters in your book. To do this, you must (a) design an invitation for the party telling what kind of party this will be; (b) tell what each character would wear to the party; (c) tell what food you would serve and why; (d) tell what kind of games or entertainment you will provide at the party.	10. Stories are made up of conflicts and solutions. Choose three conflicts that take place in the story and give the solutions. Is there one that you wish had been handled differently?	11. Imagine that you have been given the task of conducting a tour for the town in which the book you read is set. Make a tape describing the homes of your characters and the places where important events in the book took place. You may want to use a musical background for your tape.	12. Create a board game based on events and characters in the book you read. By playing your game, members of the class should learn what happened in the book. Your game must include the following: a game board, a rule sheet and clear directions, events and characters from the story.
13. Write a diary with at least seven entries that one of the story's main characters might have kept before, during, or after the book's events. Remember that the character's thoughts and feelings are very important to the diary.	14. Make a children's book retelling the plot of your book as it might appear in a third-grade reading book. Be sure that the vocabulary you use is appropriate for that age group.	15. Build a miniature setting of a scene from the book. Include a written explanation of the scene.	16. Write a scene that could have happened in the book you read, but didn't. After you have written the scene, explain how it would have changed the outcome of the book.

Independent Novel Study Contract

I choose to do the character analysis number _____

My due date for this assignment is _____

I need the following supplies for this assignment: _____

_____

_____

I choose to do the plot analysis number _____

My due date for this assignment is _____

I need the following supplies for this assignment: _____

_____

_____

I choose to do the setting analysis number _____

My due date for this assignment is _____

I need the following supplies for this assignment: _____

_____

_____

I choose to do the novel analysis number _____

My due date for this assignment is _____

I need the following supplies for this assignment: _____

_____

_____

Student signature: _____   Date: _____

Parent signature: _____   Date: _____

Teacher initials: _____   Date: _____

Middle school teacher Dennis Clark insists that students must be able to see their own interests reflected in the curriculum to feel a true sense of belonging. "Otherwise," he states, "students will say 'There's nothing for me here. I don't belong.'" Clearly that is a scenario that we can't afford. When students disengage (or worse, drop out), there is no way that they will cover the curriculum. Better is to strike a balance while students are in school, in hopes of keeping them there and of creating lifelong learners.

What Boys and Girls Choose to Write About

An area of choice making that both you and your students can immediately put into practice is reading and writing choice. You can provide your students with materials from the core curriculum, both in reading and writing, then also give them a lot of options for what to read and write. Some teachers try a 50–50 option: half core curriculum that all students read and write, half decided by the students (under fair rules set up by the teacher). If you try this option, you may well see within a few assignments how boys and girls like to make some similar and many different choices.

Biological tendencies in thinking as well as societal expectations about what is masculine or feminine influence teen choices in literature. At this delicate time of exploring their own identity, boys and girls are fitting into peer groups and being what society expects them to be, in different ways. Reading is an intimate, imaginative, emotional activity—it prompts or stimulates boys and girls differently. When we add a self-expressive component through a vehicle such as writing, boys and girls often need different prompts.

One trend you may notice is that girls often feel that it is acceptable for them to write about almost anything, including topics that are viewed as "boy topics," whereas boys generally avoid typically feminine topics. For example, boys usually avoid romance and other relationship-oriented writing. Boys in general understand this material less well than girls—they don't process the emotive material as well, and they don't notice the sensory details as well. Furthermore, as Thomas Newkirk points out in *Misreading Masculinity*, girls, more so than boys, have social permission to write about their feelings and express affection.

In general, boys will tend to be more interested—especially in adolescence—in reading plot- or action-driven stories and writing action stories filled with danger and violence, in which the characters go through an exciting experience together and triumph.

? **DID YOU KNOW? Boys Nurture in Their Own Way**

Often we as teachers are put off by boys' picking books or writing stories that include more aggression than empathy. We might not notice that sometimes boys are actually writing about their feelings and expressing emotions when they write about aggression themes. Certainly we want to help boys learn to use language to express their less aggressive emotions; it will help them in their relationships throughout their lives. But we also want to recognize and value the often male-friendly ways they express themselves.

One interesting thing you can do with both middle and high school students is to bring your "gender experiment" in choice to the students: make it a discussion starter:

Step 1. Allow choice, and record, for a month, the choices students of each gender make.

Step 2. Put the list of different gender choices up on the overhead, in two columns—boy and girl.

Step 3. Discuss it with the kids. Get them talking about gender differences, both biological and cultural.

What Do Students Say They Would Choose to Write About?

The following list was contributed by middle and high school students:

Topics and Themes Favored by Girls	Topics and Themes Favored by Boys
Girlfriends, boyfriends	Time travel
Animals	Inventions
Past experiences, memories	Mythological or science fiction creatures
Mystery	Sports
Family	War themes
Social conflict	Video games
Like to write dark poems	Movies
What is on my mind	How to do something
Dreams	World domination

As you assess student writing from the gender point of view, you may further notice that your female students tend to write more descriptively than the boys, just as they write more about verbal relationships between people. You may be tempted to see the "boy way" of writing—less sensory detail, more action; less emotive material, more action—as inferior. But given that boys naturally tend to write more about things happening and about doing things, their asset may be their ability to depict action and conflict, tension and violence, humor and edginess.

Finding where to draw the line on violence in students' writing can be challenging, especially at the secondary level. Certainly, in this era of school violence, we need to be cognizant of "warning signs" in students' writing. Writing that threatens harm to oneself or others is certainly out of bounds. Frequently, however, the violence in writing isn't targeted at anyone except a fantasy character.

As boys and girls grapple with complex issues like aggression, your giving them a safe venue to do so, such as writing, can allow them to push limits and explore their thoughts and emotions in a healthy way, and with

---

TRY THIS Choosing an American Idol

The television show *American Idol* has been a great success for a number of years—and one of the major reasons is believed to be the audience's opportunity to actually *choose* the winner. Once the initial large group of contestants is narrowed down by the judges, individual members of the audience can call in and vote for the performer they would most like to see continue in the competition and ultimately become the American Idol. This makes it crucial for the contestants to figure out who their audience is and what it wants.

You can use this popular social phenomenon as a strategy to help your students understand how to consider their audience when they are choosing a project to meet a class requirement. For instance, suppose that your various students choose to complete one of the activities from the botany class list cited earlier:

Ask each student to create a one- to two-minute "audition" of their project to present to the class (or in small groups if you have a large class). Have each student rate the audition by some agreed-on criteria: was it interesting, did it make the audience want more, did it elicit an emotional response? You can provide index cards, or index-card-size pieces of paper, that students can note their comments on and give to the presenter. If you hold these auditions early in the time frame for completing the project, students will be more motivated to think about how their audience might respond to the completed assignment.

Note: present some practice audition pieces to give the class experience with providing constructive feedback; this is an excellent opportunity for them to learn how to offer input that helps and doesn't hurt.

This activity helps students understand how to incorporate thinking about who will be reviewing their projects and how to generate interest when they choose a project. This can be a way to help students who are preparing to enter a science fair or other type of academic competition. What students learn through this activity can carry over nicely into the "real world," as there will generally be an "audience" for their work, and how they choose to present their efforts can have an impact on professional success. As a bonus, the variety of presentation styles will provide lots of novelty!

your mentoring, through your responses to their papers. Engage students in a discussion of what's appropriate, including:

- Who is the audience for the piece? A story written for grandparents or to be published on the school Web site is different from writing intended for the student's or teacher's eyes only. Pairing students who enjoy the same topics for peer editing can ensure a receptive audience for each student's writing.

- Have students determine a rating system—such as the movie rating system of G, PG, PG-13, and R—to evaluate what is acceptable for various audiences.

Using Essential Questions to Highlight Choice Making

Much of life is lived in the questions, not just the answers. Adolescents are living in the questions—questions that probe for deeper meaning and set the stage for further questioning; questions about what to choose, what not to choose; questions about choice that can foster the development of critical thinking skills and higher-order capabilities, such as problem solving and understanding complex systems. In constantly questioning, the adolescent brain is already trying to do something we want it to do throughout life; sometimes that brain just needs our help integrating and making conscious the "essential questions" it is already asking.

Do you use essential questions throughout your curriculum? They can lead to greater student success and achievement, in no small part because they tap into the student's innate and developmentally appropriate adolescent need to make choices about important issues.

What Are Essential Questions?

Good essential questions are open ended, nonjudgmental, meaningful, and purposeful; they carry an emotive force and intellectual bite; they invite an exploration of ideas. Good essential questions encourage collaboration among students, teachers, and the community, and integrate technology to support the learning process.

Many learning objectives can be reframed to create an essential question that will serve to bring increased choice making into the adolescent's learning—incorporating the student's personal strengths and interests, social interaction, and a connection to real-world issues. Many essential questions speak to boys and girls differently. From the adolescent point of view, they wouldn't be essential if they didn't.

As you integrate essential questions into your curriculum, you'll probably need to focus on creating good ones (then students can learn to write

Essential Questions to Shape a School's Curriculum

According to Kathleen Cushman in *Essential Schools Coalition,* in every class and every subject, students should learn to ask and answer these questions:

- From whose viewpoint are we seeing or reading or hearing? From what angle or perspective?

- How do we know when we know? What's the evidence, and how reliable is it?

- How are things, events, or people connected to each other? What is the cause and what is the effect? How do they fit together?

- What's new and what's old? Have we run across this idea before?

- So what? (Why should I choose to care?) Why does it matter? What does it all mean?

their own!). First, consider the focus of the unit or lesson activity. Ideas for a good essential question may stem from your students' particular interests in a topic (for example, "What makes a video game good?" "Why do you choose to play a violent video game?"), community resources ("How does pollution impact the Rio Grande River?"), local curriculum expectations ("Who was a great New Mexican leader?"), or a topic suggested by the standards themselves ("Where do waves come from?"). Next examine the theme or concept in the curriculum that must be addressed and brainstorm questions that you or the students believe would cause them to think about the concept without dictating the direction or outcome of their thinking. For example, "Why is fighting bad?" contains its own answer, namely that fighting is bad, and is the kind of question to avoid. Finally, use the six typical queries that newspaper articles address: who, what, where, when, why, and how.

Using essential questions as a driver of instruction in your classroom is a perfect way to tap into the learning differences and preferences of boys and girls. Whether students develop the essential question or work with one that you've created, essential questions are broad enough to allow students to pursue themes or strands that are most interesting to them. Further, students can gather and demonstrate knowledge in more varied ways so that all boys' and girls' abilities, interests, and talents are honored.

Once students have identified and agreed on an essential question, the next step is to formulate a list of related questions that will assist them in answering it. Often embedded within an essential question are subcategories that will generate questions that guide the students' inquiry.

For example, the essential question "Why do you choose to play a violent video game?" might lead to such subcategories as graphics, ease of use, violence, and audience appropriateness and corresponding subsequent questions, such as "How do graphics affect your enjoyment of the game?" or "How does ease of use contribute to the game's overall rating?" (This is a great time to use a graphic organizer, discussed in Chapter Three.)

In the book *Learning to Question, to Wonder, to Learn*, Jamie McKenzie provides detailed information about how to develop effective questions. It is important for teachers to learn how to develop their own based on their local content standards and their students' interests. McKenzie's book is a helpful resource for doing just that.

Essential questions can be developed across the curriculum and in fact are frequently quite multidisciplinary by nature. Here are examples of essential questions in different content areas. You will probably find that different ones appeal differently to boys and girls. You may also find that boys and girls make different choices in point of view and content as they answer these.

Language Arts

- Who was a significant hero of the twentieth century and why?
- How did a specific person or event affect the course of history?
- How are cultural values reflected in literature?
- How are the tensions of the time reflected in American literature?
- How does an author's style reflect the tensions of his or her times?

Science

- How can human activities conserve and enhance aquatic ecosystems?
- What causes global warming, and what can you do as an individual to mitigate the problem?
- How much influence do nature and nurture have on the person we become?
- Should the federal government fund stem cell research on human embryonic tissue?

Social Studies

- Should the United States of America change its foreign aid policy? Why or why not?
- How does altering the political structure of a nation affect the everyday life of its people and the day-to-day operation of its government?

- How has violence impacted our communities, and what course of action do you advocate as a solution?

- How could political issues or ideas ever become more important than family loyalties?

- Some say that our country remains wounded by the slavery experience and the Civil War. In what ways might this claim be true and in what ways untrue? What evidence can you supply to substantiate your case?

- Military officers often complain that political interference and negative public opinion on the home front interfere with their ability to conduct an effective war effort. To what extent is this true?

- Who shows greater bravery and courage in war: the frontline soldiers and the nurses who tend to the wounded and dying, or the leaders of the war effort?

Family Studies

- How could such factors as culture and gender affect world hunger?

- What impact could genetically engineered food have on our lives?

- How did various factors influence fashion and costume design during a historical time period or place?

- What causes food scarcity, and what can you do as an individual to end world hunger?

Health

- How does one's capacity to manage stress impact the body's ability to resist disease?

- What factors make someone at risk for suicide, and what kind of help is available for him or her and the people who touch the individual's life?

- What is the immediate and long-term impact of drugs on an individual, family, and community?

Three Schools in Action

Lewis Mills High School in Burlington, Connecticut, is one of three schools we feature in this section. These schools have utilized essential questions in ways that have positively affected student learning and achievement.

Lewis Mills developed the following essential questions for its course in environmental earth science:

- How is the scientific method used to acquire knowledge about global issues?

- What did John Muir mean when he wrote, "When one tugs on any one thing, he pulls on the whole world?"

- What does it mean to "think globally and act locally" (Dubois)?

Brown Summer High School in Providence, Rhode Island, offers courses based on essential questions. The school's Essential Questions courses all begin with a big question that doesn't necessarily have one right answer. Students explore the question by studying it from a variety of perspectives. Students work individually, in small groups, and as a class. At the end of the course, students show others what they have learned, not by taking a test, but more creatively, in a way that the student and teacher design together. Their course offerings read as follows:

How have science and technology changed our lives?

For the past 400 years science and technology have brought about enormous change in human society. Some people suggest that science is out of control; others argue that it must do much more. This course will explore the following questions: How does science work? Why has science been so successful? What are its limitations? How are science and technology linked? The best way to understand why science and technology have been such powerful forces for change is to work in the way scientists do: ask questions, develop hypotheses, observe and collect data, and then try to understand what we have seen and done. In this course we will do all of these activities in order to answer the questions posed above. **(Science/Biology)**

———————

What is freedom? How do you get it, and how do you keep it?

President Bush has told the American people that our terrorist enemies don't like our freedom. But what "freedom" is the President referring to: political, economic, social/cultural, religious, etc.? Using Frederick Douglass's autobiography, *Narrative of the Life of Frederick Douglass, An American Slave,* as well as other historical and contemporary materials (books, magazines, newspapers, films, music, the internet), we will examine the concept of freedom from a variety of points of view (personal, family, community, state, national and global). By the end of Brown Summer High School students will present their own ideas about "freedom" based on the reading and writing, discussion and research done in class. **(Social Studies/History)**

———————

What does the world look like through someone else's eyes?

No two people are alike. We all know that. But for many of us, it is not easy to get into other people's heads, to understand their actions, to see the world through their eyes. This class will investigate how books give us the power to stop the world and step into the minds of others. Through reading, writing, drama and discussion, we will try to answer these important questions: What does the world look like through someone else's eyes? Why is it important to understand another's point of view? How does this help us to better understand ourselves and our world? **(English)**

The Glenbrook Academy of International Studies in Illinois has developed a four-year program focused around specific essential questions that drive curriculum, instruction, and assessment. In their four years together, Glenbrook students and their teachers freely cross disciplines, cultures, and centuries. The Glenbrook faculty deems the following questions *essential* because they nurture reflection and discussion on "choice, decision making, identity, expression, perspective, change, conflict, and truth."

The following questions guide the instructional program in grade 9:

- What groups, formal and informal, do humans create and belong to? How do groups shape identity?

- Why and when did inequality among humans emerge? With what consequences?

- How did the advent of agriculture alter humankind's perspective?

- Do spiritual and material pursuits result in greater happiness or wisdom for humans?

- What are the notable achievements of "Eastern" and "Western" civilizations? Are such distinctions valid?

- What is education? What ends does it serve? What voices and groups tend to control discussion and inquiry?

Essential questions pass the "So what?" test. They are about matters of import.
    —Jamie McKenzie, *Learning to Question, to Wonder, to Learn*

Choice of Clothing in School

Many of us who went to school in the 1950s and 1960s remember hearing such slogans as "Dress right, act right." During that time, girls were generally not allowed to wear pants to school, and even boys were often not allowed to wear blue jeans. There were pretty clear rules around dress codes, and before the mid-1980s you weren't likely to see a public school requiring uniforms. In today's educational environment, there is much controversy among educators, parents, students, and even such organizations as the ACLU about whether dress codes, and especially uniforms, violate students' rights to choose what to wear.

The research doesn't really give us a clear message about the impact of clothing on the learning environment. Some individual schools and districts report that they have had decreases in behavior problems with the implementation of a strict dress or uniform policy. Some parents indicate that it makes it easier to avoid the pressure of worrying that their child doesn't have what "everyone else has," especially when that includes expensive athletic shoes or team apparel. What do the kids think? Here are some of their comments:

> "The most stressful thing for almost every teenager is all about impressing your peers. One will put amazingly important things out of one's way to show off to his/her peers. Uniforms at least take away the need to impress them with your clothes." (8th grade boy)

> "Our uniforms were supposed to make us worry less about what everyone was wearing—but now all the teachers and assistant principals stand in the hallway every day worrying even more about what everyone is wearing." (10th grade girl)

> "I believe that our school would benefit greatly from a standardized dress code, in my opinion even uniforms wouldn't be going too far. When everyone knows exactly what to wear, there is no gray area. Teachers shouldn't have to be fashion police. Their job is to teach, not to dress their students. It takes the students' minds off of name brands and latest fashions and puts it where it needs to be, in the books. Maybe then some of the students will gain some self-respect and modesty." (11th grade boy)

What's your school policy on student attire? How about the dress policy for faculty and staff? Does your school have a dress code for faculty? Does it help the adults in your environment present a more professional image and positive role model for the students? If we are going to limit students' choices of what they can wear, does it follow that there should be policies for adults too?

How you and your colleagues answer the questions about this area of choice for your students may help you evaluate how you feel about choice for students in general. Perhaps the issue of uniforms would be a good way to start a conversation at a faculty or department meeting about the options students have around choice making in your school.

Practical Strategies for Your Classroom

➡ Use the American Idol activity described earlier, or a similar strategy, to teach students about *audience* so that they can evaluate how to make project choices that will have audience appeal.

➡ Practice having students brainstorm creative ways to meet course objectives, then have them come to consensus on their top five choices. Notice if there are significant differences in the choices the boys and girls generate. Do they want to create a three-tier set of choices: a coed list, a girls' preferences list, and a boys' preference list? Perhaps they can then choose one from each of two lists. Always give the girls the option of choosing from the boys' list and vice versa. Remember that there are probably bridge brains in the group.

➡ Divide your class into an even number of teams. Let each team develop three to five choice-related issues that they think are important to teens and about which teens have serious opinions. Have them write the issues on slips of paper and then put the slips into a shoe box. Let each team draw an issue, and give the teams five minutes to outline an argument for or against the issue. Survey the class to see how persuasive the argument was.

WRAPPING UP THE MAIN POINTS

- Giving students choices not only keeps them invested in the learning but also benefits their developing brains.

- High-interest themes, topics, and genres keep students personally invested and connected.

- Making choices generates new neural connections—laying the groundwork for more efficient learning to take place.

- Choice making is something that can help in literature and literacy.

- Understanding how boys and girls write and read differently can alter the way we judge their work.

- Essential questions help guide choice making throughout the curriculum.

- Uniforms are an interesting area for discussion: Should students choose their clothes or not?

When Am I Ever Going to Use This Again?

Finding Ways to Make Learning Real

To ask questions of the universe, and then learn to live with those questions, is the way he achieves his own identity.

—James Baldwin

HAVE you ever heard students say, "Do we have to do this?" or "What does this have to do with anything?" Certainly we all learn best when we see a purpose—a connection—to the content. Isn't that why you are reading this book? You wanted to know more about effective classroom practices that help boys and girls. You sought out a book with strategies you can use, strategies rooted in the real world, strategies that are relevant to you.

Our students are looking for the same connection to reality, the same relevance. Many children are willing to do any work asked of them simply because they are asked. Girls, with a biological system that drives them to establish and maintain relationships, may have a stronger desire to please you. Boys are often less inclined to think that their classroom performance has any bearing on their relationship with the teacher, so wanting to please you in that way won't be as strong a motivation. All students can potentially approach new learning with much greater enthusiasm and retention when they see why the content matters; this sense of relevance actually creates emotional connection to the material for them.

Why Relevance Matters

Specific areas of the human brain affect motivation, and scan technologies show us that when a learning brain is motivated, more areas for learning light up. If a student cares about the content of the lesson, his or her brain more actively learns it. Of course, we all have to learn lots of things we don't care about. Being motivated to learn a particular thing is not a necessity for learning—but for most students to learn well, for their minds to light up with motivation to perform, *something* in the lesson and the classroom needs to feel relevant to them, even simply the student's belief that a piece of information will somehow help in the future.

Dr. Mel Levine, author of *A Mind at a Time,* has completed comprehensive studies on children's learning and the brain. He uses the development of good reading skills as a way of looking at motivation and relevance. He states, "The best way to learn how to read well is to read about something you know a lot about and feel passionate about. One of the ways we can leverage skills is by continually pegging them to a child's affinities. . . . An awful lot of important skills can ride the coattails of your affinities. With strengths, you begin to carve out a potential career." Levine is remarking on three of the key elements on which the learning brain of adolescents hinges motivation to learn and motivation to perform: (1) personal interest, (2) affinities and strengths, and (3) potential career.

The adolescent brain is not just growing—it's growing in a future direction. By this we mean that just soaking up knowledge is often not enough for this brain. It might have been enough when the child was seven or eight, but now, as an adolescent, the child is moving toward personal passions, inborn talents that are solidifying, an urgency to look toward what will help in the future, and a hope that what is now to be learned will be relevant to all these areas of self and potential.

Sometimes teachers who learn about the adolescent brain almost wish they hadn't! It can often seem easier just to think of these young people as sponges who should learn and perform the way we want them to. Yet all of us who teach them can remember our own need for learning to be relevant to a future, a purpose, even an affinity or passion. We remember having to "buckle down and just learn stuff because it was taught"—but don't we also remember wanting more?

School turns kids off by making them practice things they're not good at for most or all of their school day. This is especially true for those boys who do not have the verbal skills to excel in the verbally dominated classroom setting. Consider the student who is very skilled at building or inventing things, but struggles to write an essay. If science or math "goes verbal" in such a way that this learner can't feel an affinity for science and math (which are, ultimately, more calculative and spatial than verbal), we need to wonder whether something has gone wrong with our approach to adolescent learning.

Our work in schools—and the work in this chapter—is based on the idea that middle and high school educators want and need to find ways to incorporate the passions, hobbies, aspirations, and experiences of young men and young women into the life of a school. In this chapter, we'll help you gain insight and tools by which to design activities that are open ended enough to bring adolescents' interests into the classroom while still fulfilling the requirements of the curriculum. Our experience in schools of all socioeconomic groupings shows us that all boys and girls possess the capacity to become engaged and competent learners; we can tap into that capacity by building bridges between school and life.

Motivating the Male and Female Brain

We mentioned that girls are often more inclined just to do things teachers ask. There's a biological reason why. There are basic chemical differences in the male and female brain that can affect students' desire to bond with others and, through the same mechanism, to please their teachers. Oxytocin is a primary human bonding neurotransmitter and is found in higher quantities in the female brain than in the male brain. This "bonding malleability" makes females, in general, more invested in trying to please others—their teachers, their parents, their friends. Of course, the hormonal roller coaster the adolescent system is riding sometimes makes it seem that teenagers have no interest in pleasing the adults in their lives—but the truth is that the female system is, on average, more concerned with the establishment and maintenance of relationships.

Males, with lower levels of oxytocin, tend toward more aggression, greater impulsivity, and less interest in doing something simply to please their teacher. Middle school teacher Jonathan Wright contends that what matters most to the boys in his class is not earning the A or B. "Getting cool with the guys" is often the biggest reason behind what boys choose to do—or not do. "Boys need immediate feedback, and they don't often get that from the classroom teacher. Getting a laugh from their peers is the best kind of immediate feedback that many kids, especially boys, can get. And it serves a purpose that is important and meaningful to them."

"Why are we learning about polynomials?" asks an eighth grader in Val Wheeler's middle school classroom. Val notices that students—especially boys—become much more persistent in asking these sorts of questions, and it isn't always *her* response that students want to hear. In the case of the polynomials, another student, Elijah, spoke up: "Look around, dude. Polynomials are everywhere. They're in your books, in the building across the street. Learning polynomials is about access. If you learn about them, it will help you to learn and do anything you want to do in math and science. You can be what you want."

As a teacher, Val knows she's always got to be searching for the thing that helps connect kids' lives to the content she teaches. "Boys tend to poke holes in what we're doing. They question the value of what we're doing as a class. Girls don't do that as much. I guess they think, 'You're the teacher, so you must be right.'" Val has learned that often the most compelling case for learning comes from kids' questioning and challenging each other.

What Parts of the Brain Are Responsible for Motivation and Engagement?

Right ventral striatum: responsible for calculating risk and reward. This area helps people summon motivation for a task.

Oxytocin: a neurotransmitter that increases the desire to bond with and please others. Females have more oxytocin than males.

Angio-vasopressin: a neurotransmitter responsible for bonding, intermale aggression, mating persistence, jealousy, and territoriality.

Limbic system: a group of interconnected deep-brain structures involved in a number of functions, including emotion, motivation, and behavior.

Left frontal lobe: exercises conscious control over one's thoughts to allow for attention focusing, prioritizing, and problem solving.

Reticular activating system: a group of cells at the base of the brain stem that serve as the control center for attentiveness, motivation, self-control, and processing and learning of information.

"Sometimes seeing the possibilities and limitations of the real world gives kids new motivation for what they have to do in school. They see something they want, and they are more willing to jump through the hoops needed to get there. This is so much more powerful to students than having teachers tell them, 'Someday you'll need this.'"

—Rona Wilensky, high school principal

Selling the Tuna Casserole

High school science teacher Ben Boyer employs an active, humorous, and ever-changing style to make his students *want* to learn science. "I'm a salesman," he says. "I've got to sell photosynthesis or whatever it is that I'm teaching. My job is to make photosynthesis the greatest thing in the world. I want to ignite them. *I gotta sell the tuna casserole.*"

Ben does this by "changing things up" from day to day. He likes to avoid routines so that students are curious about what will happen in class and won't want to miss out. "I keep kids on their toes by changing up the way that I present." Ben knows that he is competing with the multisensory stimulation of the media world, and that can be hard for a teacher standing in front of a whiteboard. Ben gets engaged with students by walking around as he's teaching, showing excitement for the topic, getting the students interacting with each other, and weaving in references to contemporary pop culture themes. No two classes are alike. Ben calls his approach "structured flexibility," which allows leeway for building on teachable moments and pursuing students' interests and lines of questioning.

Ben uses humor whenever possible. Silly teaching analogies, such as "How the human body is like a Coke machine," serve to intrigue students and make learning more memorable. Ben likes to set the stage by telling a story that the kids can relate to, especially when it is an abstract concept such as this one:

> When I was in high school, we had Coke machines but not the kinds with the dollar bill receiver that there are now—it was quarters only then. You could stand there in front of the Coke machine with a five-, ten-, or twenty-dollar bill, but the machine couldn't use the money in that form. You had to get change made first before you could use your money in the machine (make sure the currency is in the right form, and you get your Coke).
>
> Your body is the same in that it's designed to run (get energy) on ATP only (adenazine-triphosphate, the molecule of energy) and can't accept other forms (like a dollar). When you eat different molecules as part of a meal, they each have different values of ATP that they can be converted to. Just as a five-dollar bill is twenty quarters, and so on, different molecules have different equivalencies. The body 'converts' (makes change) in the mitochondria so that the body (the Coke machine) can use it. Therefore, the body can then utilize the molecules to generate the energy to power the body.

Ben tells a great story about two teenagers cruising around town and never meeting until they both happen to stop at Taco Bell one night and see one another across the lobby. This story serves as an analogy for teaching about proteins and enzymes. When conducting yeast experiments, Ben brings in his Beastie Boys CD. The students call themselves the "Yeasty Boys" and sing together, "We must fight for our right to ferment." Boys and girls alike come to class fired up and excited because Ben is feeding their need for novelty and keeping them wondering what will come next!

Over the years, Ben has noticed that boys tend to enjoy chemistry and physics classes most. Girls tend to gravitate toward the biology and botany classes he teaches. "Maybe it's because the boys enjoy the mechanical nature of physics and like creating different mixtures and concoctions in chemistry. Girls seem to like studying living things. Either way, I have both boys and girls in my class, and I need to keep them all engaged and wanting to learn more."

One way Ben has done this is through project-based learning, which we look at in the next section.

Do what you want to do . . .
But want to do what you are doing.
Be what you want to be . . .
But want to be what you are.

—Author unknown

Project-Based Learning

One way to increase the connection between students' interests, the school curriculum, and the "real world" is to allow students to pursue project-based learning opportunities. Project-based learning switches the emphasis from teachers teaching students to students doing and learning. Students are able to exercise some choice regarding the content as well as the specific learning activities and processes. The project typically relates to a real-world problem, issue, or investigation.

One great source of project-based learning opportunities is Future Problem Solving Program International. FPSP (www.fpsp.org) offers a yearlong opportunity for teams of students to apply their problem-solving skills in their community through the Community Problem Solving challenge. Teams are divided into three levels: grades 4–6 (junior), grades 7–9 (middle), and grades 10–12 (senior).

In addition to studying a community problem, students plan a course of action and implement their plan. Teams move from hypothetical issues to real-world, authentic concerns and compete for an invitation to an international conference. A yearlong, noncompetitive component called Action-Based Problem Solving, designed for use in the regular classroom, is also available.

Student Interest Survey

Name: _____   Date: _____

Please answer these questions to the best of your ability. You may skip questions that you find to be uncomfortable.

_____

1. What is your favorite book from childhood?

2. What is the farthest point you've traveled away from home and for what reason?

3. What is a recent movie you enjoyed, and what did you like about it?

4. What is your favorite kind of music?

5. What is your favorite sport to participate in or watch?

6. To what organizations, teams, and clubs do you belong?

7. Name someone you admire and tell why.

8. What wish do you have for someone else?

9. What do you want to do for a career?

10. What is something about which you daydream?

11. What is something about which you are curious?

12. What would the title of a movie about your life be?

13. If you could go back two years, what advice would you give yourself?

14. Describe yourself as a friend.

15. Describe your best friend.

16. Respond for your own gender: What do you think a teacher can do to best meet the specific needs of boys and girls in the classroom?

17. Is there anything else you'd like to share about yourself and your interests?

Projects need to match up with students' interests relative to the curriculum. It is often very beneficial, especially in terms of motivating students, to help boys and girls match their gender interests to the curriculum.

Try using a student interest survey to get to know your students better. Information gleaned from the survey can help you guide boys and girls toward interesting learning projects. On the previous page is a sample survey that you can use as-is or adapt to meet your specific needs.

After collecting the student surveys, you might want to use an activity like Attack of the Stickies (Chapter Two) to let the students find interest areas shared by others in their class. Then let the class come to consensus on a list of topics from which to develop a project.

Social Action Projects

Young people, especially teenagers, can experience strong emotions when they see or learn of a problem in the world—whether it is pollution, homelessness, stray animals, loss of the rain forest, or bullying at their school. Emotions engage the attention and motivation of the individual and motivate people to take action. Just about any content area can have a natural tie to a social action project. The girls and boys in your class will, of course, be engaged, even entranced, by different social issues—or by the same social issue in gender-specific ways.

Building on what you have learned about how boys and girls process emotions differently, have discussions with the class that will spark both your male and female students to engage. Ask them both "how they feel" about the issue, which will likely elicit emotive responses from the girls, and "what they think" about how to address the issue, which will likely elicit more action-oriented responses from the boys and the bridge-brain girls. Both boys and girls are truly responding from their emotional center, but are generally accessing that center by traveling a different path. Encourage them to think about how both perspectives are important when addressing social issues—or issues in their own lives.

If you and your students need some help finding worthwhile projects, check out these Web sites for ideas:

Do Something (www.dosomething.org)

> Do Something is a national nonprofit organization that inspires young people to believe that change is possible, and trains, funds, and mobilizes them to be leaders who measurably strengthen their communities. It offers $500 grants to youth under thirty to implement service projects in their communities. Stop by this site for a grant application and to find out more about the many other programs the organization sponsors.

The Earth Day Project (www.earthdaybags.org)

To celebrate Earth Day, students decorate paper grocery bags with environmental messages and give them to stores to use to hold customers' groceries.

Explorers' Page (www.epa.gov/kids)

This page has a lot of interesting information about recycling, plants and animals, air pollution, and other environmental concerns.

Give Water a Hand (www.uwex.edu/erc/gwah)

Teachers can download curriculum guides that will help classes perform service-learning projects with a focus on improving local water quality.

iEarn Projects (www.iearn.org/projects/index.html)

Check out this long list of student projects organized into these areas: creative and language arts, science, environment, math, and social studies. Participants may join existing structured online projects, or work with others internationally to create and facilitate their own projects.

Kids Can Make a Difference (www.kidscanmakeadifference.org)

Kids Can Make a Difference® (KIDS), an educational program for middle and high school students, focuses on the root causes of hunger and poverty, the people most affected, solutions, and how students can help. The major goal is to stimulate the students to take some definite follow-up actions as they begin to realize that one person can make a difference. Be sure to click on the What Kids Can Do page.

Kids Care Project (http://teams.lacoe.edu/documentation/projects/windows/care.html)

This project asks students to identify a community problem and develop an action plan, including writing persuasive letters to influential people, to help combat this problem. Suggested topics include neighborhood cleanups, recycling, and tree planting.

National Service-Learning Clearinghouse (www.servicelearning.org)

The National Service-Learning Clearinghouse (NSLC) supports the service-learning community in higher education, K–12 classrooms, and community-based initiatives and tribal programs, as well as all others interested in strengthening schools and communities using service-learning techniques and methodologies. The Web site features the latest service-learning news, a searchable library catalog, NSLC publications available to order and download, bibliographies, service-learning listservs, informative how-to tool-kits, and an up-to-date calendar of events.

Wisdom of Practice: Teachers Talking

High school English teacher Tracy Brennan often discusses with students how literature relates to the world today. For instance, when her class read Orwell's essay "Shooting an Elephant," she asked her students whether the section about feeling out of place as a police officer in a foreign country that Britain was trying to rule reminded them of anyone's experience today. "When I related the question to people their own age who are fighting in Iraq, they came up with many reactions that may be felt by young soldiers in that situation."

Language arts teacher Ginny Vidulich talks regularly with students about their preferences and learning styles. She starts the year with a learning styles inventory and helps students develop self-awareness about their strengths. She tries to get each boy and girl to see how his or her self-avowed strengths will be relevant in their future workplace or family life. When students complete a project, they are allowed to utilize their strength areas to demonstrate their knowledge. Students create multimedia projects, do live performances, and set up museum exhibits. When asked how she finds time for these kinds of projects in such a crowded curriculum, Ginny responds, "The bottom line is each boy and each girl learning in a way that motivates them. Do I want to take time and make the learning memorable or rush through the content and have them only remember a small part of it? My goal is retention, and I find that thinking of relevance of learning for 'students' as well as 'boys' and 'girls' can really help."

Debra Engilman, a high school Spanish teacher at Crespi Carmelite High School in Encino, California, developed the following self-assessment to help her students better understand their own learning style. Once they have this understanding, they can use it to develop strategies for doing well in classes that don't readily suit their style. They can also identify classmates who have different styles and learn how to collaborate so that their different styles can work together to benefit both of them.

If you try this, and if your students are comfortable sharing their results, have them post stickies with their name on the board under headings for learning style. See how many students fall into each group. Have the students look for patterns between their learning styles and their gender. This might make a good discussion topic, as adolescent males and females are in the midst of trying to figure out how the other sex thinks.

Seventh-grade world geography teacher Dewey Espinoza recently taught his students about different forms of government. After discussing democracies, anarchies, theocracies, and the like, Dewey plugged in his iPod and played Pink Floyd's *The Wall* for his students. They listened to the lyrics of the song and talked about which form of government the song refers to and why. The music immediately connected the somewhat

Self-Assessment of Learning Style
(with Gender Elements Added)

Here is a learning styles inventory you can use in your class. It will help any boy or girl understand his or her learning style. It can become a fascinating starting point for discussion, both in your class and even among your faculty, when you notice the role gender plays in influencing learning style.

Name: _____   Date: _____

Read each question or statement and circle the answer that best fits you. Some will be difficult to answer, but try to choose your answer based on how you think you would most often act.

1. You usually remember more from a class lecture when
   a. You do not take notes but listen very closely
   b. You sit near the front of the room and watch the speaker
   c. You take notes (whether or not you look at them again)

2. You usually solve problems by
   a. Talking to yourself or a friend
   b. Using an organized approach, such as writing a list of steps or things to do to help solve the problem
   c. Walking, pacing, or some other physical activity

3. You remember phone numbers (when you can't write them down) by
   a. Repeating the numbers out loud
   b. Seeing or visualizing the numbers in your mind
   c. "Writing" the numbers with your finger on the table or wall

4. You find it easiest to learn something new by
   a. Listening to someone explain how to do it
   b. Watching a demonstration of how to do it
   c. Trying it yourself

5. You remember most clearly from a movie
   a. What the characters said, the background noises, and the music
   b. The setting, scenery, and costumes
   c. The feelings you felt during the movie

6. When you go to the grocery store, you
   a. Repeat the grocery list out loud or silently
   b. Walk up and down the aisles to see what you need
   c. Usually remember what you need from the list you left at home

7. You are trying to remember something, so you
   a. Try to see it happen in your mind
   b. Hear in your mind what was said or the noises that you heard
   c. Feel the way "it" felt emotionally

8. You would learn a foreign language best by

   a.   Listening to records or tapes

   b.   Writing and using notebooks

   c.   Taking a class where you would read and write it

9. You are confused about the correct spelling of a word, so you

   a.   Sound it out

   b.   Try to "see" the word in your mind

   c.   Write the word several different ways and choose the one that looks right

10. You enjoy reading most when

    a.   It's people talking to each other (a lot of conversation)

    b.   It's descriptive so you can picture the story or event

    c.   The story has a lot of action in the beginning (because you have a hard time sitting still)

11. You usually remember people you have met by their

    a.   Names (you forget faces)

    b.   Faces (you forget names)

    c.   The way someone acts, walks, or moves

12. You are distracted most by

    a.   Noises

    b.   People

    c.   The environment (temperature, comfort, and so on)

13. You usually dress

    a.   Fairly well (but clothes are not very important to you)

    b.   Neatly (in a certain style)

    c.   Comfortably (so you can move easily)

14. You can't do anything physical and you can't read, so you choose to

    a.   Talk with a friend

    b.   Watch TV or look out a window

    c.   Move around in your chair or bed

Scoring

1. Count the total numbers of answers for each letter and write them below:

   a.   _____ Auditory (learn best by hearing)

   b.   _____ Visual (learn best by seeing)

   c.   _____ Kinesthetic (learn best by touching, doing, moving)

2. Notice if one modality is a lot higher or lower, or if any two modalities are close in number.

3. Were the results as you thought they would be?

4. Which style was dominated by boys, which by girls?

abstract themes of government to something to which the students could relate. Students were challenged to think critically, take a position, and defend it. A parent of a student in Dewey's class later reported, "My son never talks about what he does in school. After that lesson, he came home talking excitedly about the lesson and could even remember what he had been taught about the forms of government!"

Val Wheeler, an eighth-grade language arts teacher, likes to engage students with literature that "really gets them going." She uses an excerpt from a speech by James Baldwin titled "A Talk to Teachers," which encourages people to challenge society's expectations. These ideas resonated with students, and they spoke passionately about how Baldwin captured their own sentiments. Val also took students to see the movie *Freedom Writers*, and now she cannot keep copies of *The Freedom Writers Diary* on the shelf. Some girls in her class told her how much they related to the female lead character and to the girl who belonged to a gang.

Wendy Pearson teaches a class strongly oriented to the real world, called Living on Your Own. After a module on child development, her high school students create a toy or game for a child and take it to a kindergarten class in the same school district in order to observe and assess the physical and cognitive development of five-year-olds. She has had older girls observe younger girls, and older boys observe younger boys; she has also switched the genders—always with fascinating results that lead to dynamic discussion.

Now is the winter of our discontent!

A Monarch High School teacher shares this story: "Making Shakespeare fun can be difficult in Intro to Theatre. We have a lesson about Shakespearean insults, where the students have a list of 'choice' words. These Shakespearean sounding words are split up into three columns. They put them together to form a full Shakespearean insult. Then we stand up in partners and yell these insults to each other using different emotions. I then have the students research for homework famous Shakespearean quotes, and choose one that speaks to them, or has meaning to them. I then have them submit theses quotes, and I type these quotes onto iron-on paper. The students bring in their own T-shirts, and we make 'MoHi Shakespeare Wear.' The students iron-on their shirts and then we designate a day where all of us wear them. It is a fun activity, and it helps with exploring the wonderful world of Shakespearean words! I have found that my students— especially the boys—retain more and learn more this way."

More Practical Ideas for Your Classroom

Here are more specific activities you can use immediately in your classroom to help connect content to your student's real world. Remember, these ideas can be translated into any content area.

Simulation Activities

Simulations engage students in ways that few other activities can. Max Fischer, author of a book of simulation activities for the social studies classroom, says, "Simulations help deliver variety to my instruction and keep students engaged to the point that discipline rarely becomes an issue."

A simulation that we've seen used successfully with all grades is a "mini-society"—an experiential unit for teaching entrepreneurial concepts that incorporates knowledge and skills from across the curriculum. Students create a town, impose taxes, create and print money. They apply for jobs in their town and file for business licenses. They purchase materials and services to produce their goods and then culminate the unit by setting up shop to sell their wares. Whether students are making change or calculating taxes and profit margins, this simulation can be as simple or as sophisticated as you need it to be. As is the case with many simulation activities, there are published units available so that you do not need to develop all the activities from scratch.

Simulations can also be specific to the events of your locale. For example, science teachers in Alaska can use simulations of the Exxon *Valdez* environmental disaster to help students develop language, math, science, and speaking skills as they engage in a court battle to represent the interests of Native nations, local governments, tourist business owners, and many other stakeholders. Math teachers in Denver can put students in the pilot's seat as they fly through the Rocky Mountains and use real-world navigation problems to hone their rate-time-distance skills and their understanding of geometry.

Simulations not only incorporate real-life situations but also offer opportunities for social interaction and friendly competition. Develop simulations that would be especially appealing to boys and others for girls, such as the following:

An issue for the girls (but everyone participates)

Before starting this simulation, pass around enough red, blue, and green stickers so that every student gets one sticker. Don't tell them what the colors represent until after they have chosen their sticker. When everyone has a sticker, tell them that people with red stickers are in favor of the issue you will present, and people with the blue stickers are opposed to the issue. People with green stickers are reporters who will be interviewing the groups. Design a newspaper headline that reads, "TENNESSEE VOTE WILL DECIDE IF WOMEN BECOME FULL CITIZENS WITH THE RIGHT TO VOTE." Date the headline May 16—the Friday before the Monday when Tennessee actually did ratify the Nineteenth Amendment to the Constitution—and post it in the classroom. Have the students form groups of "protestors" with their classmates, grouped on the basis of their red and blue stickers. Let them make

signs for their group. Have the reporters interview the groups, asking them to make their case. After all groups have had a chance to advocate for their position, have the reporters give a news report on the mood of the protestors. Then give all the students in the class a ballot and have them vote for or against ratification.

An issue for the boys (but everyone participates), suitable for a social studies, history, or language arts class

Tell your students that they are all members of the Baseball Writers' Association of America, who get to vote to decide who will be elected into the Baseball Hall of Fame on next year's ballot. Among the names up for consideration are Pete Rose and Mark McGuire. In order to be voted into the hall, these players each need as many votes in their favor as there are members of your class. Starting with the first name on the list, pass out ballots and have the class do an "informational" vote—collect the ballots and count the votes. Divide the class into those who voted yes and those who voted no. Allow each team to develop a strategy to change the other team's mind. Each team chooses a representative to make its case. After each team presentation, pass out ballots and vote again. Repeat this process three times. The vote at that point will be the final decision on the player in question. Repeat the process for each player.

These simulations can be extended over several days, giving teams time to research their issue, build their case, and develop a persuasive delivery. Following the simulation will be a great time to discuss the ethical and moral issues embedded in each topic. Because character education is something we want to have permeate our curriculum, these are great opportunities to let students engage in dialogue about character and values. These activities also provide a chance for your students to see if they noticed gender differences in how they approached each issue and worked for a resolution.

Chris Mischke, a middle school teacher, has observed,

When I do simulations (active participations) the boys' emotions always seem to run higher, especially simulations with a competitive element. Girls are the ones that tend to remain even keel. They tend to be fine with change, but do not seem to get over excited with activities outside the traditional or typical classroom setting. Boys are much more curious about how things are going to look with a non-typical day setting. Boys also prefer to get up out of their seats to work on the floor, or out in the hallway; they want space. Girls have always been better suited to stay in their seats for longer periods of time.

Video Simulations   Technology-based simulations can motivate some learners who are not motivated by more traditional activities and provide accessible ways for all students to develop intuitive understandings of abstract concepts. In a world where technology is everywhere, helping students find ways to utilize their technology interest and skills to promote learning can have far-reaching positive results—both boys and girls benefit from practice with technologies.

In a Boston College study, researchers looked at the effect of using a video game simulation to teach concepts related to electromagnetism. They found that "[f]or many students, but boys in particular, the point of the exercise was to beat the game, and the thought of replaying levels to try different strategies or learn about electromagnetism was uninteresting. For other students, many of whom were girls, the experience was less about beating the game and more about exploring the game simulation. These girls wanted to be able to record their actions, review levels, and share their results with peers."

In the video game simulation on electromagnetism, the teacher created log sheets for students to record their actions and make predictions, which reinforced the purpose of the activity and encouraged students to detect patterns in their play. The teacher also used the projector to display game levels, encouraging the class to interpret the events happening on screen and make predictions about how they thought the simulation would behave. This added structure served to focus students' play and allowed the instructor to prompt deeper reflection on game play.

Published Simulation Materials   There are a variety of published simulation activities available online. Here are a few that you might want to check out.

Stock Market Game (http://smgww.org)

> SMG is a highly successful motivational, interactive, and interdisciplinary educational program that stimulates learning about economics, finance, and the American economic system. It consists of a ten-week simulation that allows participants to invest a hypothetical $100,000 in the stock market. Appropriate for elementary through high school.

Math Quest (www.highsmith.com)

> Armed with mathematical tools and their imaginations, students travel through Numberland, Sportsland, Fantasyland, and Dinosaurland in search of great treasure. Scripted lessons introduce six problem-solving strategies that students use to earn

travel dots and accumulate gold pieces to speed their team along the Math Quest map. As they pass through seven power levels to ultimately become Einsteinians, teams face challenges posed by whimsical Fate Cards that test their preparation and ingenuity. Appropriate for grades 4–7.

Code Blue (www.highsmith.com)

You'll address your students as Doctor as they pass their board exams and become experts in the medical field. Working in cooperative learning groups, students study a specialty and teach their teammates about the inner workings of the human body through self-created visual aids. Appropriate for grades 5–8.

Skateboard Science (www.highsmith.com)

Students learn the physics of motion by designing and building a skateboard park. Appropriate for grades 5–9.

Greeks (www.highsmith.com)

Students are divided into five city-states or polises and experience the breadth of Greek contributions to our civilization. There are eight phases of the simulation covering everything from philosophy to sports. Appropriate for grades 6–12.

Discovery (www.highsmith.com)

Recreate the excitement of discovering a "new world" and facing the unknown hazards of colonizing America's East Coast in the seventeenth century. In cooperative groups, your students will practice mapping and other skills necessary to cross the Atlantic and establish a new colony. Appropriate for grades 5–9.

Civil War (www.highsmith.com)

A simulation of civilian and military life during the American Civil War, 1861–1865. In the introduction, students write journal entries, establish loyalties and discipline, and accept the simulation's point structure and responsibilities. Students become members of four Union and two Confederate units and compete for combat points in five cycles (years) from 1861 to 1865. Each cycle explores at least one significant battle (Bull Run, Antietam, Gettysburg, Sherman's march through Georgia, and Appomattox) and can be run for one or more weeks. Appropriate for grades 5–11.

Engaging Scenarios

Embedding the learning of practical skills and concepts within what are referred to as *engaging scenarios* draws learners in and makes them think, reflect, and decide. Engaging scenarios bring the outside world into the classroom. They are not as involved as simulations or essential questions, but can serve as a way to pique students' interest. Working with engaging scenarios makes learning much more interesting than just reading a textbook and writing a report without a clear sense of purpose. Engaging scenarios help students focus on the big picture and use all the knowledge they have learned, motivate students to want to get involved, and answer those questions students so often ask: "Why are we doing this?" "Why would anyone really need to know this?" and "When would I use this in my life?" And here's a major bonus: engaging scenarios can serve as built-in performance assessments.

Engaging scenarios work in any discipline. Here are a few examples, again with a range that will appeal to both boys and girls:

You have purchased a small condominium and are excited to get out on your own. You want to redecorate by painting, replacing the carpet in the bedroom and living-dining area, and replacing the kitchen floor. Because you cannot afford to make all the changes at once, you have decided to replace the kitchen floor with twelve-by-twelve-inch slate tiles and add your favorite color as a trim around the edge of the kitchen. The dimensions of your kitchen are eight feet by twelve feet. Make a floor plan of the kitchen to help find the answers to the following questions:

1. What is the area of the kitchen? Explain why you need to find the area of the kitchen.

2. How many tiles are needed to replace the floor?

3. What is the perimeter of the kitchen? Explain why you need to find the perimeter of the kitchen.

You are responsible for quality control at the Delecto Soup company. You want to make sure that materials used to make the labels meet the company's specifications. The soup can is a cylinder, and we want to cover the entire can with a label. You will need to find the area of the label, which is the surface area of the cylinder.

You have been recruited to help lead an interdisciplinary team of the 3E Pharmaceutical Company. Your team is being contracted to produce a vaccine to protect people worldwide against a possible outbreak of the avian flu. You and your teammates are now before the CEO's panel to present your results and recommendations for how to move forward. The panel members are encouraging of your work, but they also pose some tough questions, such as "What are the key points you are trying to make?" "What exactly do you want me to do about this?" "I am not convinced you understand the resource requirements of product development. Convince me." "What is your timeline? This is a quickly mutating virus." Have the student teams make their presentation to the CEO (you) and the panel (the class).

It is 1998, and the National Basketball Players Association has threatened to strike if the terms of players' new contracts are not renegotiated. Many players believe that despite their earning relatively high salaries, the National Basketball Association (NBA) is paying them unfairly. For several months, negotiations have taken place between the players and the NBA commissioner, but no agreement has been reached. The commissioner has now decided to "lock out" the players until a compromise can be reached. For many of the top-paid players, this is an inconvenience, but for a majority of players, the lockout threatens their livelihood. The NBA also has much to lose. Hundreds of millions of dollars in revenues are being lost during the lockout. Even worse, the NBA commissioner fears that a delayed or cancelled basketball season will cause fans to lose interest in the game and to resent players for appearing to be greedy. You have been called in to mediate a solution between the Players Association and the NBA. Research both parties' arguments, decide what you believe is fair, and then prepare a presentation for a joint panel of players and NBA officials.

You have graduated from college and will be relocating to the Denver area for a job. There are a number of bedroom communities from which to choose. Your new job will pay $50,000 per year, and you plan to use 30 percent of your monthly income for housing. Research communities within a thirty-mile radius of Denver and select the best community based on the cost of housing, the quality of the schools, and recreational and cultural opportunities.

You have $1,500 to cover all expenses for a trip to New York City. Plan a budget that includes hotel, transportation, food, and entertainment.

Of course, it is possible to develop engaging scenarios for any subject area. Older students can develop engaging scenarios of their own. Having your students write their own scenarios will not only test their knowledge of the subject matter but also enable you to evaluate whether or not your students grasp the central points of the lesson.

As you read through these scenarios, did you find yourself thinking, "This would appeal more to the guys in my class" or "This would more likely appeal to the girls"? Why? What was there about the scenario that made you think it would be more interesting or appealing to one gender or the other? If you want to check your intuition, offer your students a choice of scenarios and see which ones the girls and boys select. Do this with single-gender and mixed-gender groups and see if the grouping makes a difference in the choice. This information can be really helpful when you are designing scenarios and other activities that you want to appeal to all students.

Make Learning Matter with Culminating Projects

Culminating projects can help add authentic purpose to students' learning. Learning about the effects of smoking? Write letters to high school students urging them not to start the habit. Learning about recycling? Start a recycling program at the school. Studying the environment? Write letters to the local newspaper about ways to reduce pollution.

Letting students connect with the real world and a real cause will engage them emotionally in the learning. If they've had some choice in what to learn and how to learn it, they may feel quite strongly about an issue that has moral or ethical implications. Culminating projects can also be about finding ways to make a difference in the world.

The possibilities for culminating projects that can really "make it matter" for kids is limited only by one's creativity. Here are a few ideas to get you started. As you review them, think about which ones your intuition tells you would be more appealing to boys, which to girls, and which might cross gender lines and be most appealing to all students.

Letters   Have students write to the newspaper or elected officials if they wish to express an opinion or persuade the public about an issue. Students can research legislative contact information at www.house.gov, www.senate.gov, and www.capweb.net. Students can also write a letter to Dear Abby, a letter of complaint, or a letter to an author. Letter writing is an effective activity across all areas of the curriculum. Students can write to members of the armed forces stationed overseas, to local high schoolers about staying safe on prom night, to grandparents as part of a study about the students' ancestry or cultural traditions, or to a younger buddy in the school about an upcoming shared activity.

Public Service Announcements (PSAs)   Once students have identified an issue or topic, have them create a PSA directed at a character in a book or to the general public. Students can script and perform—and even film—their PSAs.

Interviews   Have students interview people who can add value to their studies. An innovative middle school teacher had her students interview war veterans. The students wove the veterans' recollections of the war into original historical fiction pieces. The veterans were then invited to attend a special reception in their honor, at which each of the students read his or her piece and the individual veteran was introduced.

Student Newspaper   Get the kids some old blazers from Goodwill, make them official-looking press badges, and have them select a school topic on which they can report. A digital camera is also a plus. A student newspaper needn't be a regular publication; it can be a one-time culminating project for a specific unit of study. Consider publishing it on the Web to save paper and copying costs.

School Improvement Project   If your students are studying measurement or geometry, perhaps their skills can be put to use to advise the school on some physical improvements. Allow students to take measurements of the grounds and create a diagram of an ideal layout of playing fields, student commons, and outdoor eating areas to demonstrate their learning of geometry and mapping skills. Other students can hone their letter-writing skills by writing persuasive letters to the director of food services about the quality of the school's hot lunches. After studying about bullying prevention, a group of students can create informational posters to hang around the school, and perform skits for other classes about how to deal with bullies.

Documentary Projects   Document learning through the use of technology! Allow students to use a digital still or movie camera and movie editing software to create simple documentary films. Nowadays, with the aid of simple Web-based tutorials, older students can work mostly independently to acquire some basic movie editing skills that will help them create simple projects.

Social Action Projects   If your students feel strongly about a topic of study, they can work to become part of the solution. Allow them to pursue opportunities to make a difference in the world in a real and meaningful way.

Web Sites   Students can create a Web site about their topic to educate others about the issue.

WRAPPING UP THE MAIN POINTS

- Students care most about learning when it can be connected to real life and real purposes.

- There is often a disconnect between students' strengths and interests and what is taught in school.

- Generally, girls are more willing to do things simply to please their teacher. This is often due to higher levels of certain neurotransmitters in the female brain.

- When teachers purposefully respect and involve students as central partners in learning, student learning improves.

- Finding out about students' interests, motivations, passions, and talents can lead to pathways by which to help students gain intrinsic motivation for learning.

- Social capital or "getting cool with your friends" is a powerful motivator for adolescents. Humor and pop culture also help make learning real and appealing.

- There are many ways to create greater authenticity, meaning, and emotional engagement for students, including project-based learning, social action projects, simulation activities, and exciting culminating projects.

Reading Between the Lines

Figuring Out What Adolescents Will Read

You've really got to start hitting the books because it's no joke out here.

—Spike Lee

WHEN we do training at middle and high schools across the country, we often hear concerned and frustrated teachers saying, "I'm not a *reading teacher*, but I spend way too much of my class period helping kids who can't read the material." The National Assessment of Educational Progress gives the United States an annual "report card" that tells us how well our children are doing in school. The 2005 report card showed that only 35 percent of twelfth graders were reading at a proficient level, defined as "demonstrating competency over challenging subject matter, including subject-matter knowledge, application of such knowledge to real-world situations, and analytical skills appropriate to the subject matter." When these data are disaggregated by gender, girls consistently show higher rates of proficiency in the literacy area. The additional verbal processing areas of the female brain are at work in creating this gender gap, which tends to open in the elementary school years and widen throughout secondary school; the gap is widened further where our classrooms are mismatched with the ways boys learn.

When reading in the content areas—that is, *reading to learn* as opposed to *learning to read*—becomes the focus in secondary education, special challenges surface for students and teachers alike. The most visible challenge is often the literacy and reading gap between girls and boys.

The Literacy Gap

We all know that reading and writing are important in many or most jobs. We all know that reading and writing are among the most profoundly

What Parts of the Brain Support Reading?

Angular gyrus: involved in the recognition of visual symbols, such as letters, words, and pictures.

Broca's area: located in the left frontal cortex and involved in language processing, speech production, and comprehension. This area is significantly involved as we learn to read because it helps us analyze new words. For skilled readers, this area is not as involved.

Occipital cortex: processes all visual information, such as the words and letters on the page.

Frontal lobe: processes the meaning of text. It helps both novice and skilled readers relate what they are reading to what they already know.

Temporal lobes: process all the sounds associated with reading. Even when you are reading to yourself, the areas of the brain that process speech are active as though you were listening to someone speak.

Cerebellum: responsible for controlling automatic eye movements and parts of the reticular formation responsible for attention.

important brain development activities in an adolescent's life. We have all probably wondered at some time or another, What is going on with the boys? Middle and high school teachers are worried about male literacy not only in the United States but all over the industrial world. In the 2003 PISA-OECD study, boys were significantly behind girls in their literacy skills in thirty-five industrialized countries.

Here are some developmental differences between boys and girls; you may recognize these patterns in your classroom and school:

- Boys tend to be a year to a year and a half behind girls in their language development.

- Boys also tend to develop reading skills later than girls do.

- More girls than boys view themselves as good readers.

- Girls gravitate toward narrative and expository texts. Boys generally prefer nonfiction and technical, work-related reading.

- Overall, boys read less often than girls. When they do read, boys are far more likely to read to get something done. Girls are more likely to read for pleasure.

- Significantly more boys than girls declare themselves to be nonreaders.

This is our starting point when looking at literacy through the lens of gender. As we've noted, some of the literacy gap is related to brain differences, and we will probably never live in a world where men read as much as women, write as many words as women, or read for pleasure as much as women.

At the same time, just as we are all committed to narrowing the gender gap in spatial technology careers—architecture, industrial engineering, physics—areas in which girls may often need more assistance, we are at a point in our society's "educational development" when we must see the literacy gap among males as an equally important issue. Much of the failure of males (higher dropout rates, lower grades, not turning in homework, higher numbers of learning disability diagnoses) is linked to nonperformance in and nonaffinity with language arts classes.

This chapter offers some solutions to the literacy gap. You'll see that many of these have been field tested and found to be successful. All are just as good for girls as boys, and some focus specifically on engaging girls, through language arts, in technology.

David Sousa's book *How the Brain Learns to Read* is a good resource that can help you really understand how to use knowledge of brain science to help your students become better readers. Once children are better readers, we can ask how we can take advantage of that skill to help them become better students in all the content areas.

Reconsidering Our Reading Lists

One of the most effective ways to help boys do better in language arts is to modify the reading lists they are provided. Many reading lists, especially those at the high school level, still comprise predominantly traditional literature that has been required reading for many years—Shakespeare, Virgil's *Aeneid*, and anthologies of classic poetry. Some of this is, of course, wonderful and necessary for all kids. At the same time, the inclusion of contemporary titles helps students feel more engaged and increases their chance of reading—and getting them to actually read is our bottom line— by mirroring issues in their own lives.

What One School Is Reading

One school adopted these reading choices for their sophomore students. All tenth graders read the following:

Frankenstein

The Wars

Catcher in the Rye

Great Expectations

Othello

Antigone

A selection of poetry

The girls read the following:

The Gardens of Kyoto (Honors)

Girl with a Pearl Earring (Regular)

The boys read the following:

Into the Wild (Regular)

Picture of Dorian Gray (Honors)

Jack London short stories (Regular)

As you peruse the lists this school designed, what do you notice about the books selected for all students to read? About the one for girls and the ones for boys? It might be interesting to share this list with your students and ask which books on the list they have read or wouldn't mind reading.

"I read philosophy, reviews of movies/music, history-related texts, and Gary Larson calendars. I read what I'm interested in."

—*12th grade boy*

"I don't like to read, but at home I read magazine articles about people I admire."

—*10th grade girl*

"I like to read and write about technology. Plus, I like to write about things that the school does not approve of, like firearms."

—*8th grade boy*

"At school, I like to read light and girly stuff. At home, I tend to read dark, harsh and sad things."

—*8th grade girl*

Meeting Gender Preferences in Reading

How can we get our reluctant readers—predominately boys—to read willingly? To see a boy immersed in a book, fingers gripping the pages, eyes widening as he is taken off guard, grimacing with surprise and horror at the text—wouldn't it be wonderful if all boys (and girls) could experience the thrill of reading?

What might you consider adding to your classroom library to be more inclusive of boys' interests and needs as readers? Use the following checklist to see if you've got a variety of reading materials available. Our guess is that your current classroom and library selections are slanted toward the preferences of girls. Think "nontraditional"!

- ☐ Both fiction and nonfiction
- ☐ Graphic novels, comics
- ☐ Music lyrics
- ☐ Texts with pop culture appeal, such as reconstructed stories from sports, TV, or movies
- ☐ Texts that reflect images of the students themselves
- ☐ Literature that exposes students to strong male or female role models who embody positive character assets
- ☐ Books in a series to get students "hooked"
- ☐ "Edgy" books—slapstick humor, violence, unexpected twists
- ☐ Action-oriented books, especially if they "start out with a bang"
- ☐ Superhero themes
- ☐ Technical how-to manuals
- ☐ Magazines of high interest (for example, video game strategy magazines)
- ☐ Newspapers
- ☐ Sports cards

Integrating Reading, Technology, and Female Role Models for Girls

Many initiatives around the country have tapped into the needs and interests of girls. One such program, Read n' Rap, is an innovative program that pairs fourth grade girls with high school girls to discuss literature through the use of technology. If you go to the program's Web site, you can see how it gets girls talking about technology pursuits and links those pursuits to literature. The program also reaches out to younger girls through novel reading and book discussions via e-mail.

Students at Muscatine High School and Franklin, McKinley, and Mulberry elementary schools in Iowa pioneered this program in 1998–99.

Check It Out: Guys Read

Guys Read (www.guysread.com) is a Web site developed by children's book author Jon Scieszka. The mission of Guys Read is "to motivate boys to read by connecting them with materials they will want to read, in ways they like to read." The following is the Guys Read mission statement:

1. Make some noise for boys. We have literacy programs for adults and families. GUYS READ is our chance to call attention to boys' literacy.

2. Expand our definition of reading. Include boy-friendly nonfiction, humor, comics, graphic novels, action-adventure, magazines, websites, and newspapers in school reading. Let boys know that all these materials count as reading.

3. Give boys choice. Motivate guys to want to read by letting them choose texts they will enjoy. Find out what they want. Let them choose from a new, wider range of reading.

4. Encourage male role models. Men have to step up as role models of literacy. What we do is more important than all we might say.

5. Be realistic. Start small. Boys aren't believing that "Reading is wonderful." Reading is often difficult and boring for them. Let's start with "Here is one book/magazine/text you might like."

6. Spread the GUYS READ word. Encourage people to use the information and downloads on this site to set up their own chapters of GUYS READ, and get people thinking about boys and reading.

Used by permission from Guys Read. ©Jon Scieszka.

In succeeding years the word spread, and several more elementary and middle schools joined the program. Through a serendipitous connection, elementary education students at the University of Northern Iowa also became involved. The project is coordinated by Mississippi Bend Area Education Agency, a regional service agency. It has been quite successful not only in helping the little girls but also in engaging the high school girls.

The girls read books chosen from a list selected by their teachers. The novels all feature strong female main characters and are at an appropriate reading and interest level for the younger girls. Historical and contemporary fiction and biographies are among the choices. While reading a particular book, the elementary and high school partners discuss the book and their reactions to it using e-mail. Some schools allow the use of free Web-based e-mail accounts; others elect to have all mail sent to the teacher's e-mail address. A moderated listserv is used to monitor the correspondence.

The mentoring and relational connectivity gained by the high school girls—to say nothing of their enjoyment of strong female role models in the books—taps into their spirit of service and their own identity development as young women, while expanding their interests, and their reading time.

Teaching with Young Adult Literature

Some secondary teachers are reluctant to teach the curriculum through the use of young adult (YA) literature. Some don't believe that it is a legitimate genre; however, these contemporary books can mirror adolescent lives in a powerful way and, at the same time, improve literacy skills. Helping adolescents make sense of their issues and concerns during a critical time in their development creates a win-win situation. In particular, YA literature

- Gives students the opportunity to view others' real-world experiences as young adults. Reading helps students empathize, see different perspectives, consider new ideas, and consider consequences of certain actions in a safe and nonthreatening way. The experiences in a book can help adolescents learn lessons without actually having to make the mistakes themselves and suffer the repercussions.

- Helps students figure out who they are and where they belong in the world.

- Models how to deal with problems teenagers face. YA books can speak to adolescents and help them sort through their own problems.

A number of teachers around the country are having success with YA literature (you'll meet a few in a moment). They have discovered that when selecting adolescent literature, they and the students must incorporate the interests of particular students (offer choice) and a variety of genres (including adventure, sports, horror, science fiction, and fantasy), point out themes of self-discovery and adolescent problems, and connect the literature to essential curricula and essential questions.

The Internet has made it easy to search for and find many lists of recommended reading—including lists developed with children's input. Every October, for example, teenagers from across the country can vote on their favorite books during Teen Read Week. For more information about how your students can participate, go to www.ala.org/teenread. The American Library Association posts an annual Teens' Top Ten list. You might find it interesting to compare these books that teens, both boys and girls, from communities across the country chose as their "best reads" to your school's list of required books. Here's the 2006 list, used by permission from the American Library Association (www.ala.org/yalsa/booklists):

1. *Harry Potter and the Half-Blood Prince,* by J. K. Rowling (Scholastic Press, 2005)

2. *Twilight,* by Stephanie Meyer (Little, Brown, 2005)

3. *Eldest,* by Christopher Paolini (Knopf, 2005)

4. *Rebel Angels,* by Libba Bray (Delacorte Press, 2005)

5. *Peeps,* by Scott Westerfeld (Razorbill, 2005)

6. *13 Little Blue Envelopes,* by Maureen Johnson (HarperCollins, 2005)

7. *Poison,* by Chris Wooding (Orchard Books, 2005)

8. *Captain Hook: The Adventures of a Notorious Youth,* by J. V. Hart (Laura Geringer Books, 2005)

9. *If I Have a Wicked Stepmother, Where's My Prince?* by Melissa Kantor (Hyperion, 2005)

10. *Elsewhere,* by Gabrielle Zevin (Farrar, Straus and Giroux, 2005)

How many of the books on this list are on any reading list at your school? If the answer is none, perhaps your language arts department could consider adding some of these titles. You might even consider conducting your own "Teens' Top Ten" survey at your school, adding the students' top titles to a section of your library that could be supplemented annually. If you choose this option, have students indicate their gender on their surveys. See how much overlap and difference there are among boys' and girls' top choices. You might also have students put stickers on the spines of books they recommend so that others who use the library could note their classmates' choices; girls and guys can use two different colors of sticker.

Also consider having your students make recommendations to other teenagers on Web sites that accept student reviews of books. This can be done at www.guysread.com, www.amazon.com, and many other sites.

The Carnegie Library of Pittsburgh has helpful section of its Web site called Kids' Page (www.clpgh.org/kids); if you click on its Book Nook and then the "booklists for fun" link on the left-hand side of the page, you will find two great lists: "Books for Boys (and Other Highly Evolved People)" and "Books for Girls (and Other Highly Evolved People)."

Teaching Reading Through Comics and Graphic Novels

Is it crazy to expand our notion of reading texts to include comics and comic books? Consider this: in countries with high youth literacy—for example, Finland and Japan—a comics culture abounds. Drego Little has studied why this is, and in *In a Single Bound: A Short Primer on Comics for Educators,* he urges teachers to "step outside the canon" and consider using comics to engage youngsters in reading and literacy. This can of course be a big step for teachers who don't consider comics to be a legitimate text and have concerns about lack of rigor.

A closer look at comics, however, reveals that they operate on a number of different levels and present stories in a way that, although appearing

How Do Comics Help Students Develop Reading Skills?

- **Assist poor readers.** Comics and graphic novels are excellent tools for use with children and young adults with poor reading skills.

- **Connect with visual learners.** As educators become increasingly aware of the importance of different learning styles, it is clear that comic books can be a powerful tool for reaching visual learners.

- **Develop strong language arts skills.** Several studies have shown that students who regularly read comic books have better vocabularies and are more likely to read above grade level.

- **Encourage unmotivated readers.** Teachers often use nonbook materials to encourage reading. Comic books are an ideal medium to spark interest, equate reading with enjoyment, and develop the reading habit.

- **Convey educational or societal messages.** Government agencies, the military, museums, and other nonprofit organizations have long used educational comics to reach general audiences. Students can learn more by researching the history of comics.

- **Stimulate readers to explore other literature.** Many comic book fans become avid book readers. Comics can stimulate interest in all types of fiction (fantasy, science fiction, historical, and so on) as well as mythology, legends, and nonfiction.

- **Engage adult readers.** The average age of American comic book readers is twenty-five. Many readers who were avid fans as teenagers continue reading into adulthood, broadening their taste in comic book genres to reflect more mature interests.

Adapted from *Comic Books for Young Adults* by Michael R. Lavin (2000); used with permission

simple on the surface, involves complex higher-level thinking. The coupling of narrative with graphics adds additional appeal for visual-spatial readers. Most of your boys and some of your girls fall into this category. Furthermore, if reader interest is important in literacy and literacy achievement, any text that appeals to millions of young readers around the world is worth considering as you develop a comprehensive classroom library.

To substitute comics for classics by Shakespeare or Harper Lee would be a step backward in education and human literacy—we all agree on that—but to integrate new literature with old (and thus get kids, especially boys, to read and write more) is a step forward.

Wisdom of Practice: Teachers Talking

Middle school language arts teacher Jonathan Wright uses graphic novels in his classroom. Recently students read a Marvel comics story about the Silver Surfer and then engaged in a Socratic seminar. Jonathan values the use of varied reading materials because he gets to see the normally reluctant or struggling students in his class come alive. Jonathan is concerned that when teachers don't use different kinds of literature in their classrooms, students will feel that their needs and interests aren't reflected at school. "If we offer only one thing, kids will think 'I don't belong here. There's not a place for me or my interests in this class.'" His success as a teacher, and his students' improvements in performance, confirm the benefits that students reap with this kind of innovative approach.

Middle school Spanish teacher Tara Koel uses comic book superheroes in a somewhat different way. When she wants students to learn months and days of the year, she has them develop a family tree. The relationship of each family member is listed (aunt, uncle, mother, father) in Spanish, along with his or her birth date. In addition, the students select a superhero character that best represents each family member and affixes the pictures next to the names. It is a simple variation, but it adds a humorous and unexpected edge to what might otherwise be a dry assignment. Creating novelty is a great way to get the brain's attention and make learning memorable!

There is no reason why the same man should like the same books at eighteen and forty-eight.

—Ezra Pound

Teachings Connecting Drama and Reading

During an eighth-grade English class, teacher Casey Banks sets up a drama exercise in place of the traditional lecture. Casey leads a discussion while in role as a character connected to the piece of literature or the topic being studied. Each student takes on a particular role and responds from that role within the discussion. Instead of being talked at to receive information, the students participate in an engaging discussion. They are having fun and learning at the same time.

That is exactly Casey's goal: to make learning matter to adolescents by connecting it to real life. Real-life connections serve to infuse learning with ethical dilemmas that engage students in concepts of right and wrong (about which they can have strong feelings!). Casey also recognizes the safety net created by allowing adolescents—who are working hard to build confidence and establish their own identities—to work "in character," instead of representing themselves.

Although these strategies work well with boys and girls who are struggling with motivation and achievement, the positive effects of creating engaging and active reading programs can be seen in even the highest-level English classes. Tracy Brennan's experience is a great case in point.

She teaches International Baccalaureate seniors at Fairview High School in Boulder, Colorado. One of the group projects her students work on is to create their own versions of *Hamlet*. One year, she had two groups of very musical students. One was a vocal group, and they created their own shortened version of the play written to a piece of music they were singing a cappella in choir. They practiced, dressed for the occasion in their medieval-style choir outfits, and gave a stunning performance of their shortened rendition of *Hamlet* to students at the neighboring middle school. Another group of students were excellent instrumentalists, so they wrote and performed their musical version of *Hamlet* without words, accompanied by explanations in the score of which scenes they were depicting through music.

All the teachers we work with who utilize drama have found the Internet to be an excellent resource for locating more information and ideas. Here are several teacher-friendly Web sites:

Using Creative Dramatics! (members.tripod.com/~ozpk/ 0000creatdrama)

> This site is a good place to start for ideas about using drama in the literature classroom. It offers a list of links for using drama to teach language arts.

National Standards for Theater Education (www.byu.edu/tma/arts-ed)

> This site provides help with using drama in the classroom. See links Grades 5–8 and Unit Lesson Plans for activities to respond to literature.

"Exploring Prejudice in Young Adult Literature through Drama and Role Play" (scholar.lib.vt.edu/ejournals/ALAN/spring95/ Bontempo.html)

> Using *Role of Thunder, Hear My Cry* as a sample, this excellent article explores different dramatic techniques to focus on cultural diversity. Using techniques of role play, improvisation, "hot seating," and tableau (freeze frame), students respond to the motives, feelings, and events depicted in several of the novel's scenes.

Middle Ideas—Puppet Shows: Animal Farm (www.teachnlearn.org/ puppet.html)

> This site displays one script by a class of students for a puppet show of Orwell's *Animal Farm*.

Readers Theater Free Sample Scripts from Storycart® Press (www. storycart.com/scripts_free.php)

> This site offers free samples of readers theater scripts. These are adaptations of pieces of literature in the form of plays for classroom use.

Monsters and Myths: Scripts (www.teachnet-lab.org/is24/pshea/
monsters.htm)

> This site is a part of a comprehensive interdisciplinary unit pairing
> language arts and the fine arts for intermediate school students.
> The lessons introduce myths and then ask students to create a
> script and perform a play.

Integrating Reading and Multimedia Tools

Today's adolescents are surrounded by media. Outside school, they constantly gather information through the television, radio, video, film, the
Internet, and more. They use a range of technology tools to communicate
with one another, including chats, blogs, instant messaging, podcasts,
social networking sites, and even online phone services.

Teachers can use these same tools to engage and motivate students and
to create new ways for students to creatively express their ideas. How can
students respond to their reading by using these tools? The possibilities
are practically limitless—and growing every day as new technologies and
applications develop.

From High School Science Teacher Ben Boyer

Last semester I wrote a grant and received funds from the Seagate Corpo-
ration for a project titled Keepin' Biology REAL (Relevant, Engaging, and
Accessible for all Learners).

My project involves the creation of weekly podcasts for my biology students to review material from my biology class in a way that is engaging
and utilizing a technology that students find very appealing, an iPod. It's
meant to be kind of like a radio show with different segments, and mixes
in some cool music. You actually don't need an iPod, just a computer with
an Internet connection. But with an iPod or any other MP3 player, the students can download the podcast and listen to it at their leisure. The idea
being that a kid is more likely to take their iPod with them skiing for the
weekend then lugging their biology book with them. Anyway, the kids can
then subscribe to the Keepin' Biology REAL podcast (www.gcast.com/user/
realbiology/podcast/main) and it will be downloaded to their computer
each time a new episode is "published." Anyone can subscribe to the podcast at the iTunes Music Store, free of charge; you can find it by searching
on the keywords "real biology."

Presentation Tools

Presentation tools, such as PowerPoint, integrate text, graphics, and animation for the creation of a sequence of slides. Multimedia presentation tools provide students with an opportunity to summarize, synthesize, and incorporate higher-level thinking skills in a format that is generally far more appealing than the standard paper-and-pencil book report or journal entry. Students can work individually or in groups. Boys generally enjoy and are motivated by the visual and technical dimensions that computer work offers. Girls may be more inclined to stick with the traditional book responses, but should be encouraged to explore and expand on their technical skills as well.

Student-Constructed Web Pages

Student-created Web pages provide a great venue for reading responses. Students can combine text, graphics, animation, Web design, and hyperlinks to put together a real-world product with a global audience for their work. Students need to collaborate and to use high-level thinking skills in order to create their own Web page.

At the secondary level, many students are already quite adept at using technology and can teach others the skills needed for Web page development. There are many Internet sites that provide helpful information on using student-constructed Web pages as a reading response strategy.

WebQuests

A WebQuest is like a scavenger hunt on the Internet. It is an inquiry-based, cross-curricular learning experience. WebQuests can motivate otherwise reluctant students to respond to literature and apply research skills. In a WebQuest, students are given a complex problem or task, and they must work cooperatively to solve it through gathering and synthesizing information from the Internet.

A WebQuest is laid out with an introduction, a description of the task, a description of the process, an evaluation, and a conclusion. WebQuests are available in all content areas and pose real-life problems, similar to engaging scenarios (discussed in Chapter Six). WebQuests take project-based learning to cyberspace. When students have a challenge to solve, boys and girls alike will read with greater purpose and enthusiasm. For a lot of your students, engaging in online reading will feel more "hip" than opening a book.

Note: because girls sometimes defer to boys when it comes to using technology, consider having students work in single-sex groups when on a WebQuest. This will allow girls to develop confidence in their technology skills without being intimidated by boys who want to jump in and take charge. Also, a single-sex group is more likely to find WebQuests that interest everyone in the group.

"Read Aloud? Aren't My Kids Too Old for That?"

Reading aloud is a commercial for reading. . . . Think of it this way: McDonald's doesn't stop advertising just because the vast majority of Americans know about its restaurants. Each year it spends more money on ads to remind people how good its products taste. Don't cut your reading advertising budget as children grow older.

—Jim Trelease

It is widely accepted that reading aloud is beneficial to young children, but no one thinks much about whether or not it might be beneficial for teenagers as well. When we think of struggling readers, however, we wonder how much they are missing by not being able to experience being swept away by a book. How many foreign lands do they never visit in their mind? How do they connect their personal experiences to the experiences of humankind? How do they appreciate how it feels to be unable to put down a book?

As we've discussed, the male brain is on average not as verbal as the female brain, and thus males are statistically more likely to have trouble in language arts learning. Generally, boys need extra support and encouragement to engage in reading. Sometimes, especially in special education classes, boys need us to read aloud to them (as do some girls as well).

Listening to stories sparks students' imaginations, allowing them to travel to other places and become other people. Here are some other advantages:

- Your inflection, pacing, and emphasis can give meaning to the text that a student might otherwise miss.

- Reading aloud strengthens the adolescent brain's ability to visualize and create sensory detail in the mind's eye, usable later in writing.

- A well-chosen read-aloud can support curriculum objectives.

- Reading aloud hones sustained listening skills.

- Reading aloud is one of the most powerful ways to get students reading independently.

Tips for Classroom Reading

- Read the book yourself before you share it with a group of students. This will give you a chance to judge the appropriateness of the language and subject matter.

- Make your listeners comfortable and close the classroom door to minimize distractions. Let students get comfortable—at their seats, on the floor, in beanbag chairs, wherever.

- Older, more experienced listeners may enjoy half-hour sessions; shorter sessions are more appropriate for younger students.

- Make this time a special treat so as to create positive associations with reading.

- Offer a peppermint for your students to enjoy while you read; studies have shown that peppermint is one of the aromas that can stimulate attention and retention in the brain.

- Pay attention to your listeners. If they're not still glued to you, it may be time to take a break.

- It's also great to time the end of the read-aloud session with a really climactic point in the book so students will hate it when you put the book down.

- Have fun. Don't try to read books you don't enjoy yourself—your lack of enthusiasm will be obvious.

More Practical Ideas for Your Classroom

Throughout this chapter, you have read about brain-based classroom strategies and ideas to enhance the reading experience for even your most reluctant readers. In this section, we want to highlight a number of ways to allow students to respond to text. Providing variety in reading responses sparks interest, increases motivation, and honors both male and female learning styles.

Verbal Responses to Reading

➡ Write a letter to one of the characters in the novel. Ask him or her questions as well as tell about yourself.

➡ Summarize the plot by creating a cartoon version of the novel. Use about six to eight frames.

➡ If you could change places with one of the characters, who would it be? Why?

➡ Create a newspaper page for one of the novels. Summarize the plot in one of your articles. Cover the weather in another. Include an editorial and a collection of ads that would be pertinent to the novel.

➡ You are a newspaper reporter whose job is to interview one of the characters. Write your interview.

➡ Write a poem about one of the novels. Touch on the characters, setting, plot, and theme.

- Develop an award for your novel. Explain the criteria for the award and why this particular book was selected to receive it. A good place to start this project is by reading about the Newbery and Caldecott awards. Notice, too, the other awards particular books have received.
- Make a time line of the events of the story. Explain it.
- Create another character for the story. Tell how things would change with this character's presence.
- Put together a display of other books the author has written. Tell about them.
- Write a Dear Abby column for all the characters in your story. Respond to their problems.
- Write a poem about the most important person in your story. Explain your reasoning for choosing that character.

Musical Responses to Reading

- Choose a familiar melody, such as "Mary Had a Little Lamb," and change the lyrics so they pertain to the novel.
- Bring in a favorite song along with the lyrics (with the expectation, of course, that the lyrics are clean!). As a class, read along with the lyrics and discuss the meaning of the song. Make connections between the lyrics and a text that the class has read recently. Conduct this activity with one student per week.
- Write out and sing songs mentioned in the book.
- Create a dance that explains the mood of your story.
- Write out and sing songs pertaining to the story.

Artistic and Hands-On Responses to Reading

- Design a front and back cover for your novel. Include the pertinent information as well as a blurb on the back.
- Create a diorama for your novel that depicts the most important scene. Write a summary of this scene, explaining its role in the story line.
- Design a story map for your novel. Include important information, such as characters, setting, and the plot. Write a brief explanation of your map.
- Make a comic book based on the book.
- Draw a movie poster advertising the story, and cast a real actor in each character's role. Explain the poster to the class.
- Make a series of five drawings depicting the major points. Describe them.
- Sew or draw a quilt square depicting an incident from your book. Put your square together in sequence with other students' squares to make a friendship quilt.

➡ Sketch a portrait of a character and write about 5–7 of the character's unique qualities.

➡ Make a map of the area where the story took place. Indicate where each event occurred and be sure to include a key.

➡ Create a mural portraying the book. Tell about it.

➡ Put together a collage of the story from magazine pictures. Describe its elements.

➡ Create a painting of a scene from the story. Tell about it.

➡ Draw a picture of your favorite part of the story. Add a caption explaining what is happening in your picture.

➡ Draw a picture time line showing the important events in your story.

➡ Make a bookmark illustrating this story. On the back of the bookmark, write at least five words you would use to describe the story.

➡ What award would you nominate this story for? Most exciting? Most likely to make you laugh your head off? Design an award for this story and explain why this story should win.

➡ Use a cereal box to tell about your book. Cover the box with paper and decorate it with the book title on the front and a short explanation of the book on the back. Add the name of the author, the publisher, and catchy phrases about the book all over the box to get people to want to read the book.

Demonstration Responses

➡ Demonstrate how to make or do something you learned from the story.

➡ Put together a display of other books the author has written. Tell about them.

➡ Prepare a recipe for a dish mentioned in the book. Show the class how to make it and give them a taste!

➡ Invent something new that you could add to the story to make it more interesting. Your invention could help a character with a conflict, change the event in the story, or . . .

➡ Make a time capsule for one of the characters. Explain what is in the capsule.

Dramatic Responses to Reading

➡ Write and perform a play based on the story.

➡ Write and perform a TV commercial to sell the book.

➡ Perform a puppet show of the story.

➡ Pretend you are a movie critic. Criticize the book as if it were a movie.

➡ Write and tape-record an interview with one of the characters in the story.

Community Service

➡ Do a community project that relates to the book. Explain it to the class.

Videography and Photography Responses

➡ Pretend you are a news reporter. Make up some stories based on the book and report on them using a video camera. Add a commercial between stories. Sell something one or more of the characters in the story would want to buy.

➡ Write and record a radio advertisement that will make people want to read the story.

➡ Write and perform a TV commercial, on video, to sell the book.

➡ Take photographs to represent someone in your story and the changes that person goes through. For example, if a character is sad all the time at the beginning of the book, you could take a picture of something blue as a symbol to represent being sad. If an event changes the character, causing him or her to feel happy, you might want to take a picture of something that makes you think of happiness. Create a photo display to present to the class.

We shouldn't teach great books; we should teach a love of reading.

—B. F. Skinner

WRAPPING UP THE MAIN IDEAS

- Generally, students spend only small amounts of time outside school reading books.

- Some students who are reluctant readers in school are actively reading such "real-world" materials as magazines, how-to manuals, Internet sites, and so on.

- Young people can learn about life, their own identity, and other issues of self-discovery through well-chosen YA literature.

- Comic books and graphic novels are often overlooked as reading texts in schools, but they do offer a number of benefits in addition to being motivating for students.

- Expanding classroom and school library selections to incorporate a wide range of reading materials and genres to appeal to both boys and girls should be a high priority.

- Consider different ways for students to respond to reading. Go beyond the standard book report fare! Technology can be a wonderfully motivating tool that opens up many more possibilities.

Modeling the Adult World

The Crucial Role of the Mentor

8

It was my teacher's genius, her quick sympathy, her loving tact which made the first years of my education so beautiful. It was because she seized the right moment to impart knowledge that made it so pleasant and acceptable to me.

—Helen Keller

A T the very time that adolescents are pushing away from adults, they need us the most. They are struggling to maintain a delicate balance between spreading their wings of maturity and independence and figuring out who they are. Adolescents often withdraw from those with whom they have been the closest in order to grow into who they will become. Of course, adolescents still need a safety net, and it is critical that parents, teachers, and other adult mentors continue to engage, supervise, monitor, and guide them. As adolescents work toward their developmental goals of separateness and detachment from parents, it can be challenging to maintain positive family relationships. This is where a caring adult outside the home can provide some of the ongoing guidance the child needs.

All of us can probably remember a teacher who deeply affected our lives. Is there one whom you can remember from your secondary school years? It was probably the teacher who provided just the right balance of high expectations and personal connection and caring. Perhaps it was someone who made you work hard but who knew it was okay to stop and laugh together. In one study, the Massachusetts Department of Education described the significant role of educators: "Possibly the most critical element to success within school is a student developing a close and nurturing relationship with at least one caring adult. Students need to feel that there is someone whom they know, to whom they can turn, and who will act as an advocate for them."

How the Brain Influences the Student-Teacher Bond

Oxytocin: helps us trust other people. When a student feels a sense of trust, his or her oxytocin level can rise, making the student more resistant to stress and social phobias. Females have more oxytocin than males and tend to trust a teacher at least minimally more quickly than a male. A male's trust often has to be earned through more action.

Vasopressin: considered to be the "male equivalent" of the receptor oxytocin. It is linked to social bonding, especially in males. Vasopressin plays a role in behavior you may have seen in class or in the halls: male bonding through contests or hierarchical jesting. You can often exploit this proclivity to build better bonds with your male students.

Dopamine: produces the rewarding and sometimes addictive effects of sex, food, and drugs of abuse. Neuroscientists believe that the same reward pathways are likely stimulated during and following pair-bond formation, including mentor-protégé bonds.

Limbic system: comprises a number of connected structures that are involved in emotional response, including the hypothalamus, amygdala, thalamus, fornix, hippocampus, and cingulate gyrus.

Consider what these students had to say about teachers they look up to:

"Ms. Passarelli was a great teacher because she challenged me to learn and be my best. We didn't get along towards the beginning of the year, but by the end, I realized that she had pushed me to learn more than many other teachers I'd had." (10th grade girl)

"My Geography and English teachers both formed direct bonds with each student. These teachers have been aware of me as an individual and given students opportunities to make the most of their abilities through very flexible projects." (10th grade boy)

"My favorite teacher is the perfect balance between friend and authority figure. She can joke with us and understand that we have responsibilities in our lives besides her class. At the same time, she is an excellent teacher and explains everything well, earning respect from her students." (12th grade girl)

"One of my favorite teachers is Mr. Peoples. I like him because he is genuine, funny and he brought fun into history. His passion for helping students is clear." (12th grade girl)

"My favorite teacher is funny and goofy. She acts like a big kid but also can get serious." (8th grade boy)

"Mrs. Gallager always asks us what we did over the weekend, how we are feeling and will always give us information on herself and how she is doing." (8th grade girl)

"My favorite teacher gets up and makes funny ways to remember things. He gets on top of desks and screams pretending to be someone else." (8th grade boy)

Why Mentors Matter

When students think of a favorite teacher, they often think about the one who relates to them personally, is interested in their lives, takes time to listen, and knows how to develop an easy rapport with students while still maintaining control of the class. One high school science teacher shared with us that he knows teachers who take on a different air as soon as they enter the classroom. Their jaw stiffens and they stand taller and more rigidly. Physically, it is as if they are steeling themselves to walk into a classroom to take control. When a teacher feels that he or she needs to gain control through a more authoritarian approach, it is harder to connect with the students on a personal level.

In his book *Teacher and Child,* Haim Ginott, an oft-cited psychologist and educator, wrote, "I've come to the frightening conclusion that I am the decisive element in the classroom. It's my personal approach that creates the climate. It's my daily mood that makes the weather. As a teacher, I possess a tremendous power to make a person's life miserable or joyous. I can be a tool of torture or an instrument of inspiration. I can humiliate or humor, hurt or heal. In all situations, it is my response that decides whether a crisis will be escalated or de-escalated or a person humanized or de-humanized."

Teachers have long recognized the importance of developing caring relationships with their students. Connecting with young people is often the most powerful motivator of learning for them. A strong teacher-student relationship can go a long way toward raising an adolescent's self-esteem, creating a caring learning environment, and promoting academic growth. In fact, one of the best predictors of students' effort and engagement in school is the relationships they have with their teachers. Some very practical thinking and strategies can help you connect and reconnect with your male and female students.

Practical Mentoring Strategies

Becoming a mentor is a very personal thing, and just because we teach does not mean we mentor. Whereas teachers are instructors of curriculum, mentors are bonded with protégés, intrinsically linked to the emotional and psychological development of the young person.

It is difficult and even invasive of "experts" to tell you or anyone else exactly how to mentor—the relationship you have with a protégé dictates the practicalities of it. At the same time, there are some very practical things to remember, and there are tools available to help you.

The Intercept Mentoring Program for Girls

Kathy Stevens was the director of the Intercept Mentor Training Program for teen girls from 1999 to 2004. The goal of Intercept was to teach eighth-grade girls mentoring skills so that they could in turn become peer mentors as they entered high school. A primary goal of Intercept was to help girls develop a culture of mentoring among themselves.

What the girls in Intercept were not told when they began was that they had been identified by their school counselor, or one or more teachers, as being in need of mentoring themselves. They were typically not girls who would have "gone for" being assigned a mentor—they were typically girls who were performing poorly academically, receiving numerous discipline referrals each grading period, being suspended from school, participating in social groups known to be involved with gangs (although the girls themselves were generally not gang members), or determined to be at

"I make an effort to learn every student's name on the very first day of class. What a difference that makes when I call on them by name instead of by saying, 'yes?' I also try to go to their performances, musical and athletic, when I can fit it into my busy schedule so that I can see them on their own turf and excelling at something other than their writing or school work. They are always appreciative, and they also like me to announce their upcoming games and competitions to the class so that other members of the class can come and support them as well. I try to spend some time working with each student individually on their writing and their oral presentations, and when we are doing a longer term project, I check in on each student to see what progress they are making, and where I can help them."

—Tracy Brennan, high school English teacher

"Ms. Trujillo is my mentor. She believes in me, even when I feel down and out. She pushes me. I really love her for who she is, and I know she feels like I'm okay the way I am."

—8th grade girl

risk for early sexual activity and teen pregnancy. The girls came from all socioeconomic and ethnic groups.

What the girls were told was that they had been recommended for the mentor training program because they had strong personalities and leadership potential, and had overcome obstacles, and thus could serve as role models for girls who were facing challenges. All these things were true. The girls did have strong personalities, developed out of a need to take care of themselves. They did have leadership potential. They had indeed overcome family and social obstacles.

Parents received a packet of information and permission forms to complete and return. The Intercept facilitator would personally contact each family (about 70 percent were single-parent families with mom as the single parent) and let them know how excited the program staff were to have their daughter as a candidate. Then each girl would be individually interviewed and given the opportunity to choose to participate. This was an important part of the program—no girls were ever *required* to attend Intercept, an important distinction for these girls in particular. Being "recommended" and having the choice to participate is very different than "being sent to" a group. Intercept facilitators had learned that this choice making was an important part of the overall high level of program completion by girls who started in eighth grade (85 percent of girls who remained in the district graduated from Intercept).

Intercept was designed based on the *best practices for girls* model of mentoring, which posits that girls are best served by a mentoring relationship that continues over a period of time. In the case of Intercept, girls were selected for the program at the end of seventh grade, and participated from eighth through twelfth grade. Led by a facilitator (a mentor) who moved to the high school with them, the girls met weekly during eighth grade and generally monthly in high school. As they became fully trained mentors, the tenth- and eleventh-grade grade girls would be assigned as mentors to peers. The girls designed their peer meetings and community projects, and led schoolwide initiatives, such as a "Kick Butts" campaign to promote resisting peer pressure to smoke. With the female adult mentors as guides and role models, the girls learned and implemented valuable lessons, developed character, and became more successful than anyone ever expected. In one school district with a 35 percent teen pregnancy rate, the girls in Intercept, who were at high risk for early sexual activity and pregnancy, had only a 5 percent pregnancy rate over six years.

During their junior and senior year, Intercept girls were paired with individual mentors, generally professional women from the community (lawyers, accountants, military officers, and teachers) who could help

---

TRY THIS Recruiting Mentors

Recruit women to be mentors for girls, and plan an evening orientation session for the women you recruit. The orientation gives the women a time to connect and develop a peer affiliation with the mentoring group of women, therein building relationships. During the evening, give the women information about the goals of your program and have them complete interest inventories and applications that spell out expectations. In today's busy world, adults are more apt to volunteer, even for a long-term commitment, if they know exactly what is expected of them.

---

the girls as they sorted out their postgraduation life plans. The girls completed interest inventories and then met the potential mentors at a group event.

For girls who did connect with individual mentors, the relationships usually continued for an average of eighteen months. Some of the adult mentors still hear from the girls as they work their way through college and start their adult lives.

There were two annual graduations held as part of Intercept. A special recognition ceremony was held at the end of eighth grade each year, celebrating the girls for all they had learned and launching them into the world of high school as skilled peer mentors ready to help other girls. Another celebration was held for the graduating seniors each year, launching them into the bigger world of life after high school. The success rate was inspiring: a graduation rate of over 90 percent and an impressive number of girls going on to college—many of whom were the first in their family to graduate from high school.

Intercept is just one of the many good models available for mentoring girls. The important thing in designing a program is to incorporate successful gender-specific guidelines. Girls Inc. has published extensively on the components of good programs designed for girls, so you might want to check out its Web site at www.girlsinc.org. If you would like more information about the Intercept Teen Mentor Training Program, visit the Gurian Institute Web site (www.gurianinstitute.com) and follow the Education Division links.

"Back when I was walking that line between being somebody and being nothing, I think I would have fallen the wrong way if you hadn't been there for me. You believed in me when I didn't believe in myself—and look at me now! I'm a teacher too, and trying hard to be the kind of mentor you were to me. I promised you I would pass it on—and I will."

—Intercept participant in a letter to a mentor

What Boys Need from Mentors

In *A Fine Young Man*, Michael Gurian explores the mentoring of adolescent boys in depth. A model introduced in that book that has shown strong results is the Core of Manhood model.

"Mr. Johnson is my chess club advisor and my mentor. He helps me to think big and to do good."

—8th grade boy

Boys often thrive on mentoring that involves *doing* things (as opposed to *talking about* things) with mentors and by connecting on important life themes. The CORE model organizes mentoring into themes:

C   Compassion

O   Honor

R   Responsibility

E   Enterprise

You can focus on these themes as you mentor an individual boy. Sentence stems and discussion starters can help:

"Did that thing you did show compassion?"

"What do you think honor is?"

"What and who have you been responsible for today?"

"What enterprising thing have you done?"

One teacher, who became a mentor to a boy named Isaiah, shared this story:

I came to one of your trainings and learned how video games, especially competitive ones, deceive the boys' brains into thinking they've accomplished something. Isaiah doesn't do his homework much, but he plays a lot of video games (three hours a day). I explained to him—he's sixteen and can understand—what was going on. "Look," I said, "think about this: you win at these video games, so the dopamine in your brain floods through it, and you think, Wow, I've done something, but actually, you've been responsible for nothing, you've done nothing enterprising, and all your honor and even your compassion is unreal, it doesn't matter much. You're sixteen," I said to him, "what's your core, what's your manhood, don't you want to be a man?"

I was pretty hard on him, and it was risky—I thought he'd turn away from me—but it actually brought us closer. This guy has never had a father: he needs direction, he needs some life themes. I told him to bring his Gameboy to my classroom, and I played games with him for about ten minutes, then I got him to help me clean up the classroom, and I got him to help me take my kids out to play ball. He wanted to become a man, he really did—he wanted to know what the core of his manhood should be. I think I had an influence on him: he didn't make it to college, but he graduated from high school, and he's in the Army, and he seems to be doing okay now.

The CORE model is only a model; it provides themes and language, but it is not meant to limit anyone. You can create any thematic model that you think will work—it is often useful to remember, as you do so, to keep repeating those themes with boys. Keep the themes relatively simple (at least on the surface), and let them be the consistent standard by which you as the mentor judge the boy's behavior.

Reaching Out to a Troubled Student

On the next page is a tool you can use to reach out to a troubled student. Try to get the student to fill out this interest inventory. Fill one out yourself as well, changing the language as appropriate. Compare the two inventories with the student, showing points of connection between you. Ask the student to talk about any or all of his or her interests with you. You don't need to cover all the interests and comparisons in one sitting.

"My mentor is like the dad I never had."

—9th grade boy

"My mentor gives me confidence."

—10th grade girl

Mentoring Parents

Whenever you as a teacher reach out to the parents of a boy or a girl, you are also opening the possibility of a mentoring relationship—not just with the adolescent but with the parents. This is a very good thing. At a time when a young person's development is filled with many physical, cognitive, social, and emotional changes, there is an increase in academic demands and in the complexity of the school structure. We all know how important parent involvement is in a child's life; we naturally want to increase collaboration between the home and school. Unfortunately, of course, many of us lack time to reach out to every parent.

A study by the Harvard Family Research Project in 2004 found that parental involvement in the form of high expectations had a measurably positive effect. "Parents who hold high expectations for their teens, communicate them clearly and encourage their adolescents to work hard in order to attain them, can make a difference in students' success." Parents of middle and high school children may need to find new ways to support students at home. Rather than helping with homework—which may be more difficult for parents once their children are at the secondary level—parents may need to offer other types of encouragement, support, and monitoring. Weekly (or, for some students, daily) conversations about long- and short-term projects, upcoming tests, current grades, and organizational strategies demonstrate the value that parents place on their child's education. Because boys' frontal lobes take longer to mature than those of girls, boys will need even more of this support. When parents get to know their child's teachers, enforce consistent rules, establish clear expectations with regard to grades, and help with postsecondary planning, they communicate volumes about their expectations and priorities.

You may need to remind parents of all this—especially if their child is struggling. You may need to respectfully mentor parents—help them reconnect with their own adolescent in specific and healthy ways.

Interest Inventory

Name: _____   Birth mo and yr: _____   Age: _____

_____

Please answer the following questions about yourself:

If you could live anywhere in the world, where would you live?

If you found $100, what would you spend it on?

How many brothers and sisters do you have?

Do you feel that you get along with your parents? If not, why not?

What types of pets do you have, and what are their names?

What school subjects do you like?

What school subjects do you dislike?

_____

Please complete these sentence starters:

_____

I do not like to . . .

I really like to . . .

If I were to describe my family as a color in art, it would be _____ because . . .

I respect people who . . .

If I could change the world, I would . . .

The animal that best represents me is _____ because . . .

Something I would like to learn this year is . . .

TRY THIS Open the Door to Parents

Creating a warm and receptive climate is key to helping parents overcome any reservations they may have about involvement at their child's middle or high school. Starting with positive assumptions about parents is key to developing positive relationships and interactions. Our attitudes and beliefs can be powerful predictors of outcomes. Lay the foundation for a productive home-school relationship with the following assumptions:

- *You and the parents have a common goal—to help the child.* You may see differently about how to accomplish that goal, but the intent is the same. Identifying the common ground can help parents and teachers collaborate more effectively.

- *All parents are to be afforded the utmost respect, regardless of their background or situation.* Every parent is treated as one would treat one's doctor or other highly esteemed individual.

- *Parents and family members are one of the best sources of information about a child.* Seek out what they know. Ask questions and listen more than you talk.

- *Parents, as do children, sometimes need special accommodations.* Parents may need more or different methods of communication, extra encouragement, such as a personal invitation to visit the class, support for behavioral issues at home, or a translator at conferences. Consider the unique needs of your students' families when you plan ways to give parents access to their child's educational program.

- *Parents want to strike the right balance between being overly involved and under involved.* Sometimes circumstances prevent parents from being as involved with school as they'd like. Other times, well-intentioned parents can hover too much or interfere. Support and communicate with parents about how to strike the right balance.

- *Concerns can be handled in a direct manner.* Both you and the parents can establish an agreement about coming to one another with issues before they escalate. It's always best to go to the source.

- *Confidentiality will be honored at all times.* Parents will open up more if they know where you stand on handling confidential information. Parents should be asked to maintain confidentiality about other children in the class.

- *Parents need to be involved in the decision-making process.* Parents are part of the team and whatever the school implements will be far more effective with support from home.

It is not always obvious to parents how they can be involved more directly at the school site. The elementary schools typically do a better job of reaching out to parents and giving them specific tasks and roles. Most often, parents of secondary school students do not receive these requests at all; however, many parents are willing to help if they know what is needed. Even if the child prefers that his or her parent not assist in his or her class, the parent could certainly assist in other class sections. Parents can also assist with tasks similar to those that they've grown accustomed to performing at the elementary school—organizing field trip forms, submitting book orders, checking homework assignments, setting up materials for a lab experiment, photocopying, and more.

Grounding Helicopter Parents

When we meet with parents as part of a school or district training, we always ask if they've heard of "helicopter parents." At our mention of these words, we can discern from the body language of some parents in the audience that they have indeed heard the term and might even be behaving a bit like helicopter parents themselves.

What is a helicopter parent? What is your role, if any, as a mentor to the adolescent who has a helicopter parent, or even as a mentor to the helicopter parent himself or herself? These are tough, even risky questions, but worth discussing in your faculty meetings, among your colleagues, and ultimately in your community. Sometimes certain parents really need you to mentor them—to respectfully help them release their adolescent boys and girls, allowing them to struggle, fail, and get up again on their own.

Here are typical stories we hear from teachers and administrators at both public and private schools:

> "If the kids forget their homework, they call on their cell phones and mom comes rushing up to school to deliver the assignment—once might be understandable, but I see the same kids calling all the time and the same moms dropping what they're doing to be a delivery driver. They may be fussing and fuming about doing it, but they do it anyway! How's that teaching responsibility?"

> "Our community tends to be economically advantaged. I've seen the local deli deliver lunches for kids who either forgot to pack lunch or didn't have money to buy lunch."

> "Kids sometimes tell me they couldn't complete a project because their parents wouldn't take them to pick up the poster board or whatever else they needed—of course, they don't seem to think there's any error in that logic when they had three weeks to do the assignment and didn't bother to ask their parents for a trip to the store until the night before the project was due."

> "I have calls from parents every time I return a writing assignment, disagreeing with a grade their kid received. Sometimes the kids seem almost embarrassed—they're OK with the grade but their parent isn't!"

When we ask parents to raise their hand if they find themselves running to the local Wal-Mart or Target at eight o'clock on Sunday night for supplies for a project due Monday, we always see a lot of sheepish parents who will willingly admit they've done just that, some more than once.

The ease of communication in today's world makes it easy for kids and parents to be continually connected. University of Georgia professor

Richard Mullendore has referred to the cell phone as "the world's longest umbilical cord," as students from elementary through high school are able to be constantly connected to parents.

More and more frequently, college administrators are expressing concern over the number of students from the millennial generation whose parents not only make the decision as to where their kids will attend college but also call their children each morning to wake them up for class, and complain to professors about grades their children have received. Many of these parents justify their overinvolvement in the college lives of their children with the excuse that they are "protecting their investment."

You may need to help these overly involved parents see that they may in fact be hobbling their child's development at a time when the child's task is to learn to be independent and self-sufficient. The seriousness of the phenomenon even extends into the business world: human resource managers tell stories of parents intruding in their children's salary negotiations and even accompanying their children to job interviews, expecting to participate!

The College Board has a page on its Web site as a resource for parents, titled "How Not to Be a Helicopter Parent." It helps parents assess whether they might be helicopter parents, describes the negative consequences of

Excerpt from "Confessions of a Helicopter Parent"

Caring for our children's welfare and helping them out along the way is a fundamental part of a parent's role, of course. But we baby boomers have made this nurturing an extreme sport. In my case, I was there in the school principal's office putting in my requests for specific teachers to ensure that my children would get the best education possible. I have constantly monitored deadlines for them, whether it's for completing a homework assignment, filing a college application, or lining up a summer job. While my husband and I have worked hard to ensure that our children are independent thinkers, we still inject ourselves into their decision-making far more than our parents did in ours. "Never leave anything to chance" has become our mantra in parenting. This involvement with our children seems right to us. Isn't this what good parenting is supposed to be, we ask? But is it healthy? Shouldn't our children be taking more responsibility for their own lives? Shouldn't we recognize that encountering obstacles and overcoming them is often a valuable learning experience? And shouldn't we back off and find something else to fill our days (and our need to be needed)? After all, most of us can expect to live at least 20 years past the time our youngest child has left the nest.

As baby boomers, we don't want to accept that we are aging, much less acknowledge our own mortality. The reality is that we will not always be there to help our children along. Will they be ready, when that day comes, to cope with whatever life brings them?

—Sarah Briggs, associate vice president of communications, Albion College this kind of parenting for their children, and discusses how they can be helpful parents without hovering. The Web link www.collegeboard.com/parents/plan/getting-ready/50129.html could supply a good bit of information to put in your next parent newsletter!

Practical Ideas for Your Classroom

What you do speaks so loudly that I cannot hear what you say.

—Ralph Waldo Emerson

Some parents are too uninvolved, some overinvolved. In your relationships with all parents, you have an opportunity to connect, gently direct, forcefully confront when necessary, and mentor. Here are some specific things you can do to mentor and gain healthy involvement from whatever kinds of parents you are working with.

➡ Have at least quarterly parent education sessions and include information on all the topics in this chapter.

➡ Invite families to share hopes for and concerns about their children and then work together to set student goals.

➡ Initiate a classroom volunteer program.

➡ Help create a parent resource center in your school. Provide materials on issues of concern to parents, such as child development, health and safety, drug education, special education, and so on. Include information about local parenting and social services agencies. If possible, provide sample textbooks, extension activities, software, and audio- and videotapes.

➡ Invite parents to present talks and demonstrations about their specialized knowledge or skills.

➡ Compile a wish list that includes both goods (consumable materials, magazines, and software) and services (stapling newsletters, chaperoning field trips, coordinating special events, and photocopying) that parents might provide. Be sure the list includes many free or inexpensive items and activities that do not demand a great deal of time or a long-term commitment.

➡ Send home parent tips for how to prepare for the parent-teacher conference and what to expect.

➡ Offer activities that allow parents to get to know one another.

➡ Accommodate parents' schedules to the greatest degree possible when scheduling conferences and special events.

➡ Have a "Take Your Parent to School Day"

➡ Organize a special outreach effort to hard-to-reach parents through telephone calls, home visits, and special mailed invitations written in their home language.

➡ Take note of the fact that more fathers are participating in school activities. Be sure to include fathers in all school communications.

➡ Hold a Grandparent's Day to honor grandparents, with special recognition given to those who have made a contribution to the school.

➡ Seek out the parents who never participate. Sometimes these parents feel inadequate or timid and simply need to be encouraged and made to feel needed.

➡ Make at least one positive phone call per week to a parent to report on a child's accomplishment.

➡ Have parents fill out a survey at the beginning of the year to tell you about their child.

➡ Follow up on problems and resolve complaints—no matter how small or insignificant they may seem. Little things have a way of building into big things.

WRAPPING UP THE MAIN POINTS

- The mentoring relationship is a special one, and goes beyond instruction.

- The brains of adolescents are hungry for mentoring.

- Some boys and girls need more mentoring than others.

- Positive role models for both boys and girls help them succeed.

- Both boys and girls respond to gender-specific mentoring.

- Troubled students often need us to forge our bonds with them by meeting them where their interests lie.

- Parental involvement during the middle and high school years is extremely important as students navigate the complex developmental challenges of adolescence.

- Helicopter parents may need our respectful help in mentoring their adolescents.

It takes two to speak the truth—one to speak, and another to hear.
                                                            —Henry David Thoreau

After the Final Bell Rings

The Lives of Teenagers Outside School

Adolescence is a period of rapid changes. When a child is between the ages of twelve and seventeen, for example, a parent ages as much as twenty years.

—Author unknown

A Pennsylvania teenager recently wrote,

> We're young, capable, and the whole world is waiting for us to take and move it and shake it in a way that no one has yet. We have every opportunity. We could become president or raise a great family. We are at the point when we can choose to do anything and reach any horizon we can get our fingers on. It's popular to doubt us, frown on us, and worry about what we're going to turn the world into. But we're teenagers, which is pretty much synonymous with being stubborn. This being true, our stubborn nature does not allow society's doubt to alter our views and aspirations. We will surprise you.
>
> Teenagers' brains are wired every which way, leaving us risky, quick decision-makers. Our passion for new things and desires can take over. I use the word "passion" because that's what we have. Teenagers are passionate about everything, whether it's writing, relationships, sports, working out, you name it, we put our all into whatever we do.
>
> We're complex, we live for the moment, and we're good at it. There shouldn't be an attempt to figure us out because, to tell you the truth, we're still figuring ourselves out. What we are learning, though, won't leave us anytime soon. Our brains capture those lessons and keep them in the backs of our minds for rainy days. Trying to define us is impossible, but just know one thing: We are America's best-kept secret.

The Challenge of Teaching (and Being) Teenagers

Your students arrive in your classroom with an amazing amount of "background noise" in their brains—a conglomeration of thoughts, emotions, hormones, and experiences. Did he argue with a sibling that morning? Is a friend not talking to her? Is he down on himself for his grades? Did she break up with her boyfriend? Is he experiencing hormonal surges that leave him feeling down or agitated? It's not every teacher who chooses to teach adolescents, but those who do get an inside view of a unique period of human development.

The stereotypical adolescent is considered to be moody, emotional, rebellious, incapable of rational thought, and prone to behavior that is often in conflict with his or her family's values and society's norms. Within the last ten years, however, researchers studying adolescent development have found that, in actuality, less than 10 percent of families with adolescents experience serious relationship difficulties and that only 15 to 30 percent of adolescents experience serious developmental problems.

This can be reassuring to both parents and teachers; however, we still sense the push-pull, the constant tug-of-war that characterizes the daily existence of adolescents as they try to reconcile their inner lives with the outside world. Therein lies the joy and the challenge of working with adolescents, as well as the compelling need to understand their lives outside school.

Although you as a teacher can't keep up with everything going on among the teenage boys and girls you teach, we want to end this book by looking at some key issues that are very much worth your attention. All these "off-campus" issues—homework, stress, sleep habits, and nutrition—have a direct bearing on the performance and discipline of both boys and girls.

Homework

Homework sucks. It makes you hate everything about school and it stresses you out. Why does it have to be that way?

—Connor, 7th grade boy

With his forehead resting dejectedly on the kitchen table, shoulders slumping, and a tone of defeat in his voice, Connor made his pronouncement. Page after page, problem after problem, he had plodded onward because he cared about getting his work done, but finally he'd had it. He expressed his feelings to his mother, and she said the only thing she could think of to say: "I don't blame you."

Many adolescents—and parents!—feel that homework is, at best, an inconvenience and, at worst, an instrument of torture. Somewhere over the course of many an evening—or in the midst of a particularly difficult assignment—any redeeming qualities of homework can be lost. Does it have to be this way?

Here are some questions you can ask about the homework you assign:

- Is it real? How does it matter?

- Does the student have some choice?

- Is there some novelty involved?

- Does it provide any opportunities for competition?

- Can it be done on the move?

Check out these homework assignments. How do you think your students might react to them? Will the boys and girls react differently? Why? If you feel it is appropriate, open a discussion with your students about the value of these kinds of homework assignments. Note the comments from your boys and your girls. See where they have similar or different views of what kind of homework would be most helpful to them.

- As a **writing** assignment: students write up a review of their favorite video game, giving some reasons why playing the game would be a positive leisure-time activity for teens.

- As a **math** assignment: students play a dice game (such as Yahtzee) and project probabilities of throwing a certain dice combination. You could design a worksheet to go along with possible throws of the dice and have students record the number of times each is thrown and chart those numbers.

- As a **social studies or history** assignment: students interview a family member or other adult who lived through an important historical event (for example, the assassination of John F. Kennedy or Martin Luther King, the *Challenger* disaster, the World Trade Center attack). Students play the role of a reporter in the major news media and write a column, record an interview, or do a video clip of the interview.

- For a **foreign language** assignment: students imagine they have pen pal in a country that speaks the language they are studying. They can send their pen pal a recipe for their favorite dish. Have them write up the recipe with all needed instructions.

- For a **biology assignment**: students make a set of "Just the Facts" cards to illustrate vocabulary words for the unit they are studying. They write the word on one side of the card; on the opposite side, they draw a

"The best teacher I ever had did homework really different. At the beginning of a unit she would give us a chart with all kinds of possible ways to earn homework credit. Like there were maybe 20 different things we could choose from, but we only had to do, say 12 by the end of the unit. At least some of the 12 would be fun things so it made it easier to do the ones that were less fun. You could turn them in in any order and for most units you could actually earn extra credit by doing additional assignments. I think that was the only class I ever had where I never missed turning in homework."

— 10th grade boy

picture or paste one from a magazine that they believe represents the word. The next day in class, students can quiz each other, trading partners so that everyone gets to see everyone else's cards. The cards can then be used for study and review.

How Boys and Girls View Homework Differently

Researchers have found gender differences in homework management practices that indicate that your male students are more likely to experience problems. Writing in *Educational Psychology*, researcher Jianzhong Xu found that, compared to boys, girls on average report spending more time doing homework, are less likely to go to class unprepared, and consider homework to be less boring. With what you've learned already about the differences in boys' and girls' brain structure, chemistry, and function, these findings probably don't come as a surprise. Your innovations in the area of homework benefit both male and female students, but can be absolutely pivotal for your low-performing boys.

If you're interested in finding ways to make homework more engaging and relevant, consider the Teachers Involve Parents in Schoolwork (TIPS) "Interactive Homework" assignments developed by John Hopkins University. These assignments require students to talk with someone at home about a question, issue, or project that is connected to what students are learning in class. Often, these activities move beyond having students ask for help with an activity and get family members involved in contributing to the activity. In this way, families are discussing subject matter with students and finding out more about what they are learning at school. More information about TIPS interactive homework, including sample activities and blank templates, can be found at www.csos.jhu.edu/p2000/tips/TIPSmain.htm.

Interactive homework assignments are especially good in areas where you wish to increase parent-child communication. For example, middle school health teacher Sue Kendall has students and their parents discuss and respond to questions about tobacco, alcohol, appropriate dress, curfew, and sexual activity. Some of the questions that parents and students respond to include "Should students be allowed to wear revealing clothes?" "Should alcohol be illegal for everyone?" "Why is a college education all that important?" This homework gets conversations about real-life issues started in the home—conversations that might not have otherwise taken place if it had not been for the assignment.

Of course, not all homework assignments can be project oriented or emotionally engaging or hands-on. It's good, however, to establish some basic parameters that serve as your guide in developing homework assignments of all types. Consider the following suggestions when assigning homework:

- Ensure that students understand the goals and purpose of all homework.

- Never assign homework as a form of punishment.

- Assign homework that builds on lessons taught in class.

- Practice a few problems in class so that students have no good reason to go home and say, "We've never done this before."

- Take time at the end of class to make sure students have written down the complete assignment.

- *Require* the use of an assignment notebook.

- Make sure parents understand your expectations for homework so that they can support and monitor its completion with an appropriate amount of support.

- Always stress *quality* not *quantity* when developing homework assignments.

- When possible, give students some choice about homework—not in terms of whether or not they will *have* homework, but in terms of *what* their homework is.

- When possible, select homework activities that will be fun for students to do. For example, instead of having students do traditional homework problems or assignments, try some of the suggestions in this chapter.

Understanding that boys have a tougher time accepting the intrinsic value of homework, pay special attention to their need for assignments to have relevance.

How much weight do you give to homework when calculating your student's grades? Do you consider neatness, turning all assignments in on time, and even whether assignments are completed in pen or pencil or typed on a computer? For your students who are active in class, get good grades on homework they do turn in, and get good grades on tests, does missing homework ever cause them to get a lower overall grade? Take a look at the information in the following box for some interesting research on how homework is especially affecting our boys.

A week has gone by, and seventh grader Connor is back at the kitchen table working on his homework, but tonight the scene is different. He starts his homework without prodding from his mom this evening, and instead of working from a textbook, he's using an "Evolution Lab" online simulation (at www.biologyinmotion.com/index.html) to develop a better

"I try to get them started on their homework, especially the more difficult assignments, while we are in class together, and then let them go from there. I always give them a weekly or monthly plan so they know what homework is coming up and what to expect when. That way, they don't get overwhelmed with work in one class, and can parcel out their work for my class."

—Tracy Brennan, high school English teacher

Smart Boys, Bad Grades

A report by Julie Coates and William Draves, 2006

Available atwww.smartboysbadgrades.com/smartboys_badgrades.pdf

LATE HOMEWORK: A MAJOR CAUSE OF THE GPA GAP

A major reason for the GPA gap is homework. If you look at boys' work, their test scores are fairly equal with girls. It is homework where boys overall fall well short of girls. We looked at grades of one or more boys using an online grading system. The online grading system, which is able to separate test from homework components of a grade, showed higher grades for tests. Only homework dragged down the grades. We also confirmed this with interviews with dozens of boys. We also did a random survey of 200 K–12 teachers across North America. Some 84% said boys turn in homework late, only 4% said girls. Another 8% said neither, and the final 4% said they did not know. A second question asked whether turning homework in on time would improve the students' homework scores. Some 96% said yes, only 4% said no. Thus, K–12 teachers confirm that boys turn in homework late more than girls, and that boys are penalized for turning in homework late.

---

understanding of the essential elements of the process of natural selection. He follows the directions for setting the cycles and mutation rates to see how his creatures evolve.

Is Connor more alert and engaged in his homework on this evening? Yes. Is he now "sold" on the idea of homework? No way. He still thinks that homework is not a good idea. "It stresses kids out and is bad for their self-esteem," he asserts. When asked why homework is bad for self-esteem, he replies, "Well, when kids don't do their homework it makes them look bad to their teacher and then they lose their self-esteem." At this point, we're all probably thinking, "So just do your homework then!" but it's not always that simple. The more we can do as teachers to make homework less rote and more interactive, less drill and more engaging, the better. The less painful homework is perceived to be, the more students will complete it—and that's a win-win for everyone.

Practical Ideas for Dealing Better with Homework

➡ Provide families with a list of required mastery skills for each subject.

➡ Create a classroom Web site and include a parent page.

➡ Set up a "homework hotline" that students can call to get forgotten or missed assignments. Remember, the goal is to put the responsibility on students while helping parents resist the urge to hover.

➡ Inform parents of how and when they can contact you at school. Provide your direct number and be specific about the best days and times to reach you. Let parents know how often you check e-mail during the day so that they know how soon they can expect to receive a response.

➡ Send home via e-mail a weekly overview of what you're doing in class.

➡ In collaboration with you and their parents, have students set goals for organization, work completion, and grades.

➡ Communicate early and often if a student is struggling in any area.

Stress in the Lives of Adolescents

Stress? Well, I'd say peer pressure, homework, lack of sleep, parents. A lot of things are stressful.

—10th grade girl

In a McLean Hospital study at Harvard University, Susan Andersen and her colleagues found that social stress during adolescence (ages approximating thirteen to fifteen years in humans) showed a significant decrease in a specific protein found in the hippocampus, a brain region important for learning and memory. These preclinical data are the first to demonstrate that stress experienced during adolescence can alter the normal developmental trajectory of the hippocampus, but that these changes are not apparent until later in life.

Young people become stressed for many reasons. Some forms of stress are beneficial, such as wondering how your classmates will respond to your valedictory speech at graduation. Some are general life stressors that can occur at any age, such as being the victim of a natural disaster or worrying about terrorism. Some are more typical of the developmental stage of adolescence (or more intense), such as problems with friends, breakups with boyfriends or girlfriends, and increased conflict with parents. Whatever the stress, the body and brain go through physical and psychological responses that can affect learning performance and discipline.

And as in so many things, boys and girls experience some of their stress differently, with somewhat different consequences.

Gender and Stress

In a study conducted by the American Psychological Association in 2006, a stress gap between the sexes was confirmed: 51 percent of women reported that they were stressed compared to 43 percent of men. Other studies have confirmed similar results—women score significantly higher than men for chronic stress in their lives. Females also have a much higher incidence of depression. One current theory about this is related to higher levels of estrogen in the female brain. As you have learned in this book, cognitive functions are affected by hormones, such as testosterone and estrogen, in the brain. Similarly, these hormones may change the brain's sensitivity and response to stress. Beginning at puberty, significant differences between males and females emerge in the area of stress and stress management.

Writing in *Psychology Review,* researchers from UCLA analyzed data from hundreds of studies, concluding that females were more likely to deal with and manage stress by "tending and befriending"—that is, nurturing those around them and reaching out to others. Males, in contrast, were more likely to sequester themselves or initiate a confrontation, behavior in line with the fight-or-flight response that has long been associated with stress.

The researchers found that oxytocin, a hormone that promotes both maternal and social behavior and enhances relaxation, is most likely the key factor behind the gender difference. Initially, women have the same response to stress as men, leaving them somewhat vulnerable to the stress hormone cortisol and the aggression-producing adrenaline. After a short period, however, women also begin secreting oxytocin from the pituitary gland, which helps scale back the production of cortisol and adrenaline, minimizing aggression. Interestingly, men also secrete oxytocin when under stress, but they produce it in smaller amounts than women do, and its effects are inhibited by the dominant male hormone, testosterone.

What the Kids Say Stresses Them

"I hate the way cliques fight with each other. It's the cool kids vs. the chess club, the drama club vs. basketball. It sucks being caught between them." (8th grade boy)

"Hard classes and social life are probably tied for the most stressful things in a teenager's life." (10th grade boy)

"The pressure that parents put on their kids is too much." (12th grade girl)

"Pressure to smoke or do drugs." (6th grade boy)

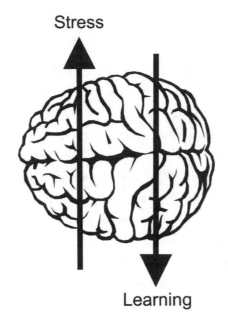

Stress

Learning

Practical Ideas for Helping Teens Deal with Stress

→ Establish a relationship with students early on in the school year or semester so that they feel comfortable talking to you when they need to.

→ Regularly use humor in your class—laughing releases endorphins into the body that can help promote good health and lower stress.

→ Have reasonable homework expectations.

→ Make sure that your class provides a secure environment with structure, stability, and predictability.

→ Make sure your students have regular access to water—drinking water has been shown to reduce cortisol levels.

→ Encourage students to use relaxation techniques, such as physical exercise, music, deep breathing, visualization, neck rolls, stretching, and other noninvasive stress busters.

→ When appropriate, play soothing music in class and have students take deep calming breaths. Try this right before students take a test and see if the decrease in stress hormones doesn't help them perform better.

Early to Bed, Early to Rise?

Have you noticed some of your students dozing off in class? Can you tell they are not sleeping enough? Just when biological changes associated with puberty change the circadian rhythm (the biological clock) of adolescents, school start times often shift to earlier in the morning. Most adolescents are sleep deprived, as are many younger children and adults in today's hectic world. Increasingly, brain research is showing that our school scheduling

? **DID YOU KNOW? It's About Sleep!**

Researchers used to believe that adolescents' desire to sleep later was caused by late nights of school activities, homework, socializing, or computer use. Now they've discovered that adolescents actually need more sleep per night than adults—and that the onset of sleep naturally occurs later. As males and females enter later puberty, the pineal gland, deep in the brain, secretes the sleep-related hormone melatonin later at night than it did during childhood—up to several hours later. This makes it often difficult for teenagers to go to sleep until between 11:00 P.M. and 1:00 A.M., even if they've gone to bed at a reasonable hour. Unlike adults who start to feel sleepy as the evening wears on, adolescents can be wide awake and fully alert. When a teenager tells his or her parents "I'm really not sleepy," it's probably the truth.

Studies also show that adolescents may experience greater physical difficulty rising in the morning. The American Psychological Association reports that teens require 9.25 hours of sleep per night, although they rarely get that much (on average, 6.5 hours per night) and end up chronically sleep deprived. Catching up on weekends doesn't do the trick and can actually result in other sleep-related problems.

Unfortunately, when your students arrive sleep deprived in your classroom, you are faced with a roomful of teenagers who may be suffering from impaired memory and inhibited creativity. Sleep-deprived students are often more irritable and depressed, with decreased ability to engage in problem solving and a greater propensity for mood swings. Sleep deprivation can also interfere with the functioning of the immune system and put students at greater risk for becoming ill.

policies are in direct contradiction with the biological needs of adolescents. You may have planned the most exciting lesson of all time yet see it fall flat, because while your students' bodies are in their seats, their brains are back on the pillow at home. As a classroom teacher whose first period begins at 7:30 A.M., you are working against Mother Nature, and the impact on learning may show.

Gender and Sleep

Across all age groups, insomnia is reported more frequently by females than by males. Studies have shown that females have greater difficulty maintaining sleep, feel less refreshed in the morning, and experience more frequent excessive daytime sleepiness. Females also report that they need more sleep than males report. Scientists have found an association between anxiety and many sleep disturbances; however, after making adjustments for many factors, including gender and psychological health, the gender differences mentioned remain significant. With more brain activity as a result of greater blood flow, a larger number of neural connections between areas of the brain, and a tendency to be engaged in multitasking—a brain that won't shut off!— women seem to be more likely candidates for sleep problems.

In contrast, sleep apnea (cessation of breathing during sleep), is more common among males. Apnea produces loud snoring and may actually interfere with the sleep of other family members. It leaves sufferers sleepy during the day and places them at greater risk of getting into an automobile accident; it also compromises their ability to learn, due to lack of ability to stay focused. Scientists have now learned that higher levels of estrogen and serotonin in the female's system result in greater control of the tongue during sleep, resulting in a lower incidence of blockage in the upper airway.

Proper sleep helps ensure students' physical health, as well as optimal brain functioning at school and in life. Often parents do not explicitly discuss these issues with their children. You can help by providing students with practical tips, such as avoiding caffeine after noon (and in general); avoiding stimulating TV shows, music, and computer games close to bedtime; and dimming the lights in the evening to support the secretion of melatonin.

Reconsidering School Start Times

As we have already pointed out, middle and high school students who have the greatest biological need to sleep later are the ones who typically start school the earliest. There are lots of reasons why school districts, parents, and even teenagers have resisted a later start, including time pressures related to school bus transportation, after-school jobs, child care for younger siblings, and sports and other extracurricular activities. Some school districts, however, have found a way to make brain-friendly changes in their start times.

Edina, a suburban school district just outside Minneapolis, changed its high school start time from 7:20 to 8:30, and the Minneapolis Public Schools changed their start time from 7:15 to 8:40. This provided a unique opportunity for Kyla Wahlstrom and a research team from Center for Applied Research and Educational Improvement to collect information from teachers, parents, and students about the resulting effects on work, sleep, and school habits. Despite having the typical "late start" concerns, 92 percent of parents in Edina indicated that they preferred the later start time after one year of implementation. Data from Minneapolis schools showed that there was a significant reduction in school dropout rates, less depression, and higher grades.

Carol Johnson, superintendent of Minneapolis Public Schools, says, "We have received feedback from many families and staff affirming our decision to use these data to reorganize school times, and the data have resulted in many other districts in the state and around the country changing start times to better match students' learning rhythms with the school's instructional program."

News of Edina's success is spreading. Marilyn Conner, administrative consultant to Mesa County Valley School District no. 51 in Grand Junction, Colorado, points to the Edina research as pivotal in the decision to change school start times in that district.

Perhaps your school district is one of the many that already looking into the issue. Some school districts, such as the Boulder Valley School District in Boulder, Colorado, started by making a smaller and logistically easier change. The district changed the elementary and middle school start times so that most elementary schools start at 8:00 and most middle schools start at 8:45. The high schools still have an early start, but the district took at least a step in the right direction for some of its adolescent students.

When it's not possible to implement school start time changes right away, what can schools do in the meantime to help sleep-deprived teens? As much as possible, schedule first-period classes that include movement and whole-brain activity, classes like physical education, art, music, and drama. Although teachers of these subjects need their students awake too, their content areas engage the brain in a more active way, helping "wake up" that brain power and get it moving in the morning.

Practical Ideas Regarding Sleep

➡ Talk to your students about the importance of sleep and give them tips for proper "sleep hygiene" so that they develop good habits for a lifetime.

➡ During your first- and second-period classes, it will be even more important to engage students in movement and social interaction. Use upbeat music to energize students when they come into the room. Incorporate plenty of brain breaks so that they don't fall asleep on you!

➡ Get students involved in debates or discussion about controversial issues. Engaging their emotions will wake up their brains.

➡ Consider allowing students to bring a snack (or their breakfast, if they haven't already eaten it) to class to ensure that their blood sugar isn't bottoming out.

➡ Share information with your students about the harmful effects of caffeine on the developing teen brain—too many adolescents are using coffee and other high-caffeine drinks to help them wake up—a dangerous alternative to adequate rest.

They Are What They Eat

As young people gain greater independence from their parents, they begin to make more and more of their own decisions, including decisions about what to eat. Unfortunately, typical adolescent eating habits include

? **DID YOU KNOW? A Good Breakfast Can Be Crucial to Learning**

We can't overestimate the brain-friendly nature of breakfast for teen boys and girls. The brain is much like a car: it needs fuel to run, and it will run more efficiently when it is given a higher grade of fuel. Students who don't eat breakfast are more prone to headaches, stomach cramps, irritability, poor concentration, and fatigue. Students who skip a meal for the purpose of dieting actually increase their chances of overeating later in the day. Studies show that eating breakfast is associated with

- Improved physical performance
- Strength and endurance in the late morning
- Increased alertness and attentiveness
- Increased concentration
- Better performance on tests
- Improved grades

increased meal skipping, snacking, consumption of fast foods, and dieting. Students are not only prone to nutritional deficiencies but also failing to establish the eating habits that build the foundation for a healthy lifestyle. Brain research has shown that poor nutrition contributes to unhealthy brain development, behavior problems, and learning difficulties.

Poor eating habits can also be linked to other issues over which you as a teacher may at first seem to have little or no control. For instance, when adolescents have to get up and get ready for school while their body is still in a sleep phase, they can find it difficult to eat a good breakfast or any breakfast at all. Their hunger alarms haven't kicked in because their body isn't "awake" yet. So they come to your school both asleep and not having "broken their fast." Later in the morning, probably during their second- or third-period class, they will get really hungry! But it's not yet lunchtime, so their bodies are apt to get physically stressed as they respond to hunger, another state that doesn't make it easy to focus on biology or literature or algebra.

Gender Issues and Nutrition

Girls usually experience their adolescent growth spurt between the ages of eleven and fourteen, although as we know there is great variation among individual girls. Boys, in general, experience their growth spurt later, between thirteen and sixteen.

The most common deficiency among both boys and girls during this period is iron—needed for building lean body mass (muscle). By the end of adolescence, boys tend to have double the muscle mass of girls, who turn more carbs (or sugars) into fat than muscle. Furthermore, as girls become more concerned about maintaining or losing weight, they often eat more vegetables, which are not bad for them, but are limited in iron, in lieu of iron-rich foods. Iron matters, and kids need to know.

Because 90 percent of the adult skeletal mass forms by age seventeen, it is also critical for adolescents to get adequate amounts of calcium during the teen years. Girls, more at risk for osteoporosis later in life, tend to be more susceptible to calcium deficiencies; less than 20 percent of adolescent girls get the recommended daily amounts of this nutrient.

Overall, teenagers' diets tend to include lower than recommended levels of nutrients—lower for boys than for girls—and higher than recommended amounts of sugars—higher for boys than for girls. Furthermore, fast-food diets are like an epidemic among our teens. These diets are significantly high in fats. No good for either boys or girls, these diets can especially lead to obesity and weight issues for girls. Soft drinks, high in sugar and caffeine, can harm boys and girls; already physically impulsive boys becoming even more so after the caffeine and sugar intake.

As a teacher, you certainly can't control what and when your students eat. You can, however, educate adolescent boys and girls about the importance of developing a healthy "man's body" and "woman's body." Here are some nutritional components you can build into your lesson plans. You can add a gender dimension to each of these by having boys and girls focus the assignment on their own gender.

- As a **math** assignment: students calculate the amount of calories in a variety of foods on the cafeteria lunch menu, along with the amount of activity it will take to burn that amount of calories.

- As an **economics** assignment: give every student a "food budget" for one week and challenge them to actually shop and make a list of the foods they could buy and prepare that would be high in nutrition and low in fats and sugars. After all the menus are turned in, have the students vote on a favorite meal and plan a class "feast." See if there are differences between the genders.

- As a **reading** assignment: students read *Fast Food Nation*, by Eric Schlosser, and debate the issues raised in the book. Boys and girls will have similar but also distinct perspectives.

- As a **social studies** assignment: watch the movie *Super Size Me* as a class and talk about the culture that promotes fast-food eating. This movie can stimulate good general discussion, and you can also divide the students into single-gender groups and then have the groups report back to the whole class. It can be fascinating to see what the girls focus on and what the boys focus on.

Practical Ideas Regarding Nutrition

You can do some things immediately to try to help students eat better:

➡ Keep water available.

➡ Keep protein bars available (be careful with food allergies).

➡ Think about letting kids eat a quick bite before first or second period—if they've had no breakfast.

➡ Talk with students about their breakfast choices that day.

➡ As they enter their first class, have students write their initials on a food pyramid to show which food groups their breakfast came from.

➡ Have students identify breakfast foods they like and plan out a breakfast menu for the week.

➡ Talk to students about the importance of nutrients to build neurotransmitters for the brain and the impact that healthy brain development has on learning.

➡ Have students record their breakfasts for a month and record how they feel each day once they are in class.

➡ Contact your school administrator or district's food services department to propose the establishment of a healthy snack bar that is open during the morning hours.

If you are a health teacher, these activities are a perfect fit for a health curriculum. At the same time, you can use these in any class. If nutrition becomes a daily topic for the first five minutes of the school day in any classroom, students will become not only more knowledgeable but also more conscious of their food choices each morning.

WRAPPING UP THE MAIN POINTS

- The high levels of turmoil and conflict stereotypically associated with adolescence are actually not the norm for all teens.

- Homework can be beneficial for students as long as it is of high quality, involving the application of skills in meaningful contexts.

- There are differences in male and female attitudes about homework, and the two genders differ in terms of organization and completion of homework. Boys tend to be less motivated to do their homework, which leads to lower grades.

- Assigning motivating, interactive, and hands-on homework increases the likelihood that the homework will get done and students won't get turned off.

- Help your students understand the importance of adequate rest. Teens don't sleep enough—in some part because of school start times—and can often perform less well academically as a result.

- Adolescence is a stressful time. Students need to be taught coping mechanisms and have support systems in place.

- Boys and girls experience and respond to stress differently. Understanding these brain-based differences can help you recognize and respond more effectively to students in distress.

- Good nutrition can be crucial to academic performance and good discipline.

Epilogue

I N our travels, we gather the stories of teachers and students from near and far. And although the circumstances and the kids vary greatly, the stories are remarkably similar. There are adolescents—not all adolescents, but far too many—who are disconnected, disengaged, disinterested. School learning does not awaken their soul; rather, it seems to deaden it. Teachers' souls, too, are deadened as they become disconnected from the reasons they became teachers.

Everywhere we look, we can find discouraging statistics about adolescents. Secondary education as a whole is awash in reform initiatives as old paradigms are reexamined. And although there is a shared hope among all school reformers that our young people will be engaged, successful learners, most of the reform efforts do not honor and address the core nature and hard-wired biology of our adolescents.

As educators (and as parents, siblings, and spouses), you get it! You've observed and experienced firsthand the very basic differences between how our boys and girls see and interact with the world. The training that we do all over the country reinforces that you and thousands of other teachers are asking for the same thing: the knowledge and skills to weave together the science of the brain and the art of classroom practice to help both boys and girls flourish in your classroom.

Thus we are filled with hope. We are energized by the growing tide of teachers' passion for understanding how boys and girls learn differently and by their desire to transform their classrooms. We share teachers' excitement as they start to come alive again as teachers . . . finding joy in teaching and delighting in their students' learning. They understand that in the delicate dance between teacher and student, the student must be allowed to lead. The curriculum must take a backseat to the child. *There—we said it (in unison with so many of you)!* If we want academic success and engagement for our students, we must follow the pathway laid by *who they are*—the passions, the hobbies, the hearts, and the biology of our young people.

With this book, we have endeavored to provide for you exactly what you've told us you need. It is our hope that this blend of cutting-edge brain science and extensive and practical information about classroom strategies has helped you weave together the art and science of teaching. We also hope that you have marveled at the wonders of the human brain (as we do!) and have identified many new strategies to implement right away in your classroom. We also wonder whether you recognized some of the strategies and activities in this book as things you are already doing. We hope you did! Teachers have tremendous experiential knowledge about what works with kids. We challenge you, then, to think more deeply about your current teaching practice—what you do, how you do it, and why you do it—so that you can be more intentional and more informed in your instructional decision making.

Ultimately, we hope that all of you have developed a profound respect for the unique qualities that all adolescent students, both male and female, bring to the classroom. With this book, we've endeavored to open up a new way of thinking about your students and your classroom. One classroom at a time, teachers have the power to change that powerful yet delicate dance . . . to tap into the hearts and souls of students and, in so doing, to reconnect with the true purpose and joy of teaching.

Sources

Chapter One

Baron-Cohen, S. (2003). *The essential difference: The truth about the male and female brain.* New York: Basic Books.

Blum, D. (1998). *Sex on the brain: The biological differences between men and women.* New York: Penguin Books.

Carter, R. (1998). *Mapping the mind.* Berkeley: University of California Press.

Jensen, E. (2000). *Brain-based learning: The new science of teaching and learning.* (Rev. ed.) San Diego, Calif.: Brain Store.

Jensen, E. (2006). *Enriching the brain: How to maximize every learner's potential.* San Francisco: Jossey-Bass.

Moir, Anne, & David Jessel. (1992). *Brain Sex: The Real Difference Between Men and Women.* New York: Delta.

Rhoads, S. E. (2004). *Taking sex differences seriously.* San Francisco: Encounter Books.

Salomone, R. C. (2003). *Same, different, equal: Rethinking single-sex schooling.* New Haven, CT: Yale University Press.

Sousa, D. A. (2001). *How the brain learns.* (2nd ed.) Thousand Oaks, CA: Corwin Press.

Wolfe, P. (2001). *Brain matters: Translating research into classroom practice.* Alexandria, VA: Association for Supervision and Curriculum Development.

Chapter Two

Evanski, J. (2004). *Classroom activators.* San Diego: The Brain Store.

Gurian, M. (2002). *Boys and girls learn differently!: A guide for teachers and parents.* San Francisco: Jossey-Bass.

Gurian, M., & Stevens, K. (2004, November). With boys and girls in mind. *Educational Leadership, 62*(3), 21–26.

Gurian, M., & Stevens, K. (2005). *Minds of boys.* San Francisco: Jossey-Bass.

Jensen, E. (2000). *Learning with the body in mind.* Thousand Oaks, CA: Corwin Press.

Jensen, E. (2001). *Teaching with the arts in mind.* Alexandria, VA: ASCD.

King, K., & Gurian, M. (2006, October). Teaching to the minds of boys. *Educational Leadership.*

Sprenger, M. (1999). *Learning and memory: The brain in action.* Alexandria, VA: ASCD.

Chapter Three

Gould, R., Duey, K., & Epstein, E. (2000). *The time soldiers series.* Big Guy Books.

Gurian, M. (2002). *Boys and girls learn differently!: A guide for teachers and parents.* San Francisco, Jossey-Bass.

Gurian, M., & Stevens, K. (2004, November). With boys and girls in mind. *Educational Leadership, 62*(3), 21–26.

Gurian, M., & Stevens, K. (2005). *Minds of boys.* San Francisco: Jossey-Bass.

Hawkins, J. (2006, October). Think before you write. *Educational Leadership.* 63–66.

Helmstetter, S. (1995). *What is self-talk. The Self-Talk Solution.* Retrieved from www.selftalk.com/index.html

King, K., & Gurian, M. (2006, October). Teaching to the minds of boys. *Educational Leadership.*

Porter, K., & Foster, J. (1990). *Visual athletics.* Dubuque, IA: Wm. C. Publishers.

Sprenger, M. (1999). *Learning and memory: The brain in action.* Alexandria, VA: ASCD.

Chapter Four

Applebee, A. N. (1996). *Curriculum as conversation.* Chicago: University of Chicago Press.

Dee, Z. *Team Building.* Retrieved from the World Wide Web: www.sonoma.edu/kinesiology/ppep/experts/team.htm

Department of Geosciences at Oregon State University. Volcano World. *A Collaborative Higher Education, K-12, and Public Outreach project of the North Dakota and Oregon Space Grant Consortia.* Retrieved from the World Wide Web: http://volcano.und.edu/vwdocs/msh/llc/is/cl.html

Harvey, D. (2002). What are literature circles? *Literature Circles.* Retrieved from the World Wide Web: http://www.literaturecircles.com/article1.htm

Kennesaw State University. (2006). Kennesaw State University Educational Technology Training Center. Retrieved from the World Wide Web: http://edtech.kennesaw.edu/intech/cooperativelearning.htm#elements

Kihn, L. Establish a positive community atmosphere in your classroom through team-building activities. *Teachers Network: Who We Are.* Retrieved from the World Wide Web: http://www.teachersnetwork.org/ntol/howto/start/teambuild.htm

McLaughlin, M. W., & Talbert, J. E. (2001). *Professional Communities and the Work of High School Teaching.* Chicago: University of Chicago Press.

Schick, B. Classroom Interpreters–Interpreters and Children–Cognitive/Social Development and Educational Interpreting. *Classroom Interpreting.* Retrieved from the World Wide Web: http://www.classroominterpreting.org/Interpreters/children/Cognitive/index.asp

Schlick, N., Katherine, L., & Johnson, N. J. (1999). Getting Started With Literature Circles. Christopher-Gordon Publishers.

Wilhelm, J. (2002). *Action Strategies for Deepening Comprehension.* New York: Scholastic Inc.

Chapter Five

Cushman, Kathleen. Asking the Essential Questions: Curriculum Development. *Old Horace,* vol 5, no. 5, June 1989. Available at: http://www.essentialschools.org/cs/resources/view/ces_res/137#figure1

McKenzie, J. (2005). *Learning to Question, to Wonder, to Learn.* FNO Press.

Newkirk, T. (2002). *Misreading Masculinity: Boys, Literacy, and Popular Culture.* Heineman.

Wormeli, Rick. "Differentiating for Tweens." *Educational Leadership.* April 2006. Vol 63, no. 7. p. 14–19.

Wormeli, Rick. (2005). *Summarization in any subject: 50 techniques to improve student learning.* Alexandria, VA: ASCD.

Chapter Six

Bache, J. *Adults read, kids succeed. Read aloud Virginia.* Retrieved from www.readaloudva.org/partnerschools/res_classtips.htm

Cushman, K. Asking the essential questions: Curriculum development. *Old Horace, 5*(5), June 1989. Retrieved from www.essentialschools.org/cs/resources/view/ces_res/137#figure1

Pennac, D. (2006). *Better than life.* Coach House Press.

Stallworth, B. J. (2006). The Relevance of young Adult Literature. *Educational Leadership, 63*(7), 59–63.

Wilhelm, J. (2006, April). The Age for Drama. *Educational Leadership, 63*(7), p. 74–77.

Education Development Center, Inc. (EDC). *Criteria for selecting adolescent literature.* Literacy Matters. Retrieved from www.literacymatters.org/adlit/selecting/criteria.htm

Chapter Seven

Barrett, V. D. *Book Report.* May/June 2000 issue.

Baron, M., & Rude, S. *Comic Books and Reading.* Retrieved from http://ublib.buffalo.edu/libraries/units/lml/comics/pages/reading.html

Callenbach, E. (1990). *Ecotopia.* New York: Bantam.

Green, D. (2006). Welcome to the House System. *Educational Leadership, 63*(7), 64–67.

Kaiser Family Foundation. (March, 2005). *Generation M: Media in the lives of 8–18-year-olds.* Retrieved from www.kff.org/entmedia/7251.cfm

Little, D. (2005, March). *An a single bound: A short primer on comics for educators.* New Horizons for Learning. Retrieved from www.newhorizons.org/strategies/literacy/little.htm

Lavin, M. (2000). *Comic books for young readers.* Retrieved from http://ublib.buffalo.edu/lml/comics/pages/reading.html

Moloney, J. (2002). *Ideas for getting boys to read.* Retrieved from www.cbc.org.au/qld

National Middle School Association. (2003). *Research and resources in support of This We Believe.* Westerville, OH: National Middle School Association.

Eisner, W. (1985). *Comics and sequential art.* Tamarac, FL: Poorhouse.

McCloud, S. (2000). *Reinventing comics: How imagination and technology are revolutionizing an art form.* New York: Perennial Currents.

McCloud, S. (1994). *Understanding comics: The invisible art.* New York: Harper Perennial.

Myers, B. R. (2002). *A reader's manifesto: An attack on the growing pretentiousness in American literary prose.* New Jersey: Melville House Publishing.

New London Group (1996). A pedagogy of social multiliteracies: Designing social futures. *Harvard Educational Review, 66*(1), 60–92.

Norton, B. (in press). *The fantastic motivating power of comic books: Insights from Archie comic readers.* Reading Teacher.

Sanford, K. & Blair, H. (2003). *Canadian Adolescent Boys and Literacy Study.* Boys and Literacy. Retrieved from www.education.ualberta.ca/boysandliteracy/findings.html

Chapter Eight

Battistich, V., Solomon, D., Watson, M., & Schaps, E. (1997). Caring School Communities. *Educational Psychologist*, 32:3 (1997): 137–151.

Bryk, A. S., & Schneider B. (2002). *Trust in Schools: A Core Resource for Improvement.* New York: The Russell Safe Foundation.

Felner, R., Favazza, A., Shim, M., & Brand, S. (in press). Whole School Improvement and Restructuring as Prevention and Promotion: Lessons from Project STEP and the Project on High Performance Learning Communities. *Journal of School Psychology.*

Luks, Allan & Payne, Peggy. *The Healing Power of Doing Good.*

Pianta, R. C., & Hamre, B. K. (2001). Students, Teachers, and Relationships Support (STARS). Lutz, Fla.: Psychological Assessment Resources.

Kidron, Yael & Fleischman, Steve. (2006). Promoting Adolescents' Prosocial Behavior. *Educational Leadership.* 63(7), p. 90–91.

Miller, F. (1994). Gender differences in adolescents' attitudes toward mandatory community service. *Journal of Adolescence, 17*(4), 381–393.

Smith, Thomas. (April 2005). Ethnic and Gender Differences in Community Service Participation Among Working Adults. *Journal of Extension.* Vol 43, no. 2. Available at: http://www.joe.org/joe/2005april/rb1.shtml

Trudeau, K. J., & Devlin, A. S. (1996). College students and community service: Who, with whom, and why? *Journal of Applied Social Psychology, 26*(21), 1867–1888.

Chapter Nine

Aidman, A. (1995). Advertising in the schools. *ERIC Digest,* ED389473.

American Psychological Association. (2006). Connections between stress and unhealthy mind/body choices. Stress and Mind/Body Health (News Release). Available at: http://apahelpcenter.mediaroom.com/index.php?s=pageA&item=1

Boqard, K. (Summer 2005). Affluent adolescents, depression, and drug use: the role of adults in their lives. *Adolescence.*

Carpenter, S. (2001). Sleep deprivation may be undermining teen health. *Monitor on Psychology.* Vol 32, no. 9. Available at http://www.apa.org/monitor/oct01/sleepteen.html

Pollan, Michael. (2001). *Botany of Desire: A Plant's Eye View of the World.* Random House.

Brain Briefings. (February 2003). *The Society of Neuroscience.* Available at: http://www.sfn.org/skins/main/pdf/BrainBriefings/BrainBriefings_Feb2003.pdf

Centers for Disease Control and Prevention, Division of Nutrition, Physical Activity and Obesity. (2007). *Fast Food in Schools.* Available at: http://www.cdc.gov

Eller, D. (2000). Stress and Gender. *WebMD Feature.* Available at http://www.webmd.com/a-to-z-guides/features/stress-gender

Evanthia N. Patrikakou. (September 2004). Adolescence: Are Parents Relevant to Students' High School Achievement and Post-Secondary Attainment? *Harvard Family Research Project Digest.* Cambridge, MA: University of Illinois, Chicago, and Mid-Atlantic Laboratory. Available at: http://www.gse.harvard.edu/hfrp/projects/fine/resources/digest/adolescence.html

Guilfoy, Christine. (2006). Researchers Look To The Brain To Explain Gender Differences In Sleep Apnea. *Medical News Today.* American Physiological Society. Available at: http://www.medicalnewstoday.com/medicalnews.php?newsid=40979

Herscher, E. (2006). Stress and Gender. *Lifestyle and Wellness.* Available at http://healthresources.caremark.com/topic/stressgender

Holmbeck, G. N. (1996). A model of family relational transformations during the transition to adolescence: Parent-adolescent conflict and adaptation. *Journal of Early Adolescence.* 1996. pp. 167–199.

Wahlstrom, Kyla L. (1999). The Prickly Politics of School Starting Times. Kappan, Vol 80, no. 5, pp. 344–347.

Walker, J. (2002). Adolescent Stress and Depression. *Teens in Distress Series.* University of Minnesota. Available at: http://www.extension.umn.edu/distribution/youthdevelopment/DA3083.html

Xu, J. (2006). Gender and Homework Management Reported by High School Students. *Educational Psychology.* Vol. 26, no. 1, p. 73–91.

Index

A

Adobe Photoshop, 53

All-subject-area activities, 27–29; Attack of the Stickies, 29, 93; Ball Toss Review, 28; Finger Spelling, 28; Musical Chairs, 28; Scavenger Hunts, 27–28; Vote with Your Feet, 29; Walking Review, 28; Who's Got Talent?, 29

Amen Clinics, 14

American Library Association, Teens' Top Ten list, 114–115

Amygdala, 7; and choice making, 71

Andersen, Susan, 147

Angio-vasopressin, and motivation/ engagement, 89

Angular gyrus, and reading, 110

"Anytime" brain breaks, 26–27; Cross-Laterals, 26; Deep Breathing, 26; Do the Wave, 27; Gotcha!, 27; Hand Fidgets, 26; Making Contact, 27; Mirror Image, 27; Standing Up, 26–27; Stretch!, 26

Are You Right? activity, 31

Artistic and hands-on responses to reading, 123–124

Attack of the Stickies activity, 29, 93

Attention: part of the brain responsible for, 71; and reward, 19

B

Back on the Job activity, 30

Baldwin, James, 87, 98

Ball Toss Review, 28

Banks, Casey, 117

Baron-Cohen, Simon, 14

Biology assignment, as homework, 143–144

Blood flow, in the brain, 8

Boy-girl learning differences: chemical differences, 10–12; developmental paths, 3; learning styles, 1; processing differences, 8–10; right/left hemispheres of the brain, 12–13; science of, 1–16; structural differences, 4–8

Boyer, Ben, 55–56, 65, 90, 119

Boys: aggression vs. empathy, 7–8, 75; blood flow in the brain, 8; dopamine in, 11–12; fight or flight response in, 6; language processing areas, 8–9; and movement while learning, 17–18; and multitasking, 6; and oxytocin, 12; processing of verbal and emotional information, 8; processing/response to classroom information, 5; retention in, 7; right-hemisphere preference, 13; and sensory processing, 9–10; serotonin levels, 11; spatial processing areas, 9; testosterone, 3, 10, 62, 148

Boys and Girls Learn Differently! (Gurian), 13, 15

Brain: growth of, 88; motivating, 89; and social functioning, 62

Brain-body connection: activities for any subject area, 27–29; "anytime" brain breaks, 26–27; common teacher questions/concerns, 21–25; language arts activities, 29–30; mathematics activities, 30–32; maximizing, 17–37; physical movement, importance in learning, 17–20; practical ideas for the classroom, 25–36; practice, wisdom of, 20–21; science activities, 32–35; social studies activities, 35–36

Brain integration, 19

Brain stem, 6

Breakfast, importance to learning, 153

Brennan, Tracy, 20, 54, 64–65, 95, 117–118, 129, 145

Brenner, Pam, 56
Bridge brains, 14
Briggs, Sarah, 137
Broca's area: and reading, 110; and social functioning, 62
Brown Summer High School (Providence, Rhode Island), use of essential questions by, 82–83
Build It activity, 67
Build It II activity, 67

C

Carnegie, Andrew, 62
Carnegie, Dale, 17
Carnegie Library of Pittsburgh Web site, Kids' Page, 115
Cell Scrambler activity, 34
Cerebellum, 5; and reading, 110
Cerebral cortex, 4–5
Chemical, 10–12; dopamine, 11–12; estrogren, 10–11; oxytocin, 12; serotonin, 11; testosterone, 10
Cherry Creek PREP Alternative High School, 20
Choice making, 69–85; American Idol, choosing, 77; choice of clothing in school, 83–84; classroom strategies, 85; independent novel study contract, 74; and learning, 70; novel analysis, 73; novel choice activities, 72; part of the brain responsible for, 71; teachers' role in, 71–75; three schools in action, 81–82; using essential questions to highlight, 78–83; what boys and girls choose to write about, 74
Circulation and respiration, 19–20
Civil War (simulation), 102
Clark, Dennis, 74
Classroom Quilt activity, 67
Classroom reading, tips for, 122
Classroom Rules activity, 57
Clue Scramble activity, 35
Clue Sort activity, 35–36
Coach's playbook, as model, 40–41
Coates, Julie, 146
Code Blue (simulation), 102
Collaborative learning, 60–61
Comics and graphic novels, 57; teaching through, 115–116
Compass Rose Run activity, 35
Conceptual organizers, 46–47

Conner, Marilyn, 152
CORE model, mentoring, 131–133
Corpus callosum, 6; and visual-spatial thinking, 45
Cross-Laterals activity, 26
Cruger, Gregg, 55
Culminating projects, 105–107; documentary projects, 106–107; interviews, 106; letter writing, 106; public service announcements (PSAs), 106; school improvement project, 106; social action projects, 107; student newspaper, 106; Web site creation, 107
Cyclical organizers, 48

D

Dance Through the Ages activity, 36
DaSilva, Ed, 49
Dee, Zack, tips on teambuilding, 63
Deep Breathing activity, 26
Demonstration responses to reading, 124
Depression, 148
Detective activity, 67
Developmental differences between boys and girls, 110
Digital movies, 53
Digital skills, 53
Discovery (simulation), 102
Distress, 20
Do Something (www.dosomething.org), 93
Do the Way activity, 27
Documentary projects, as culminating project, 106–107
Donley, Kristin, 54
Dopamine, 11–12, 44; and student-teacher bond, 128
Dramatic Reenactments activity, 33, 36
Dramatic responses to reading, 124
Draves, William, 146
Drawing to summarize, 57
Drawings, 49–52; creating on the computer, 53

E

Earth Day Project, 94
Economics assignment, nutritional components for, 154

Einstein, Albert, 25

Emerson, Ralph Waldo, 138

Emotional Intelligence (Goleman), 60

Engaging scenarios, 102–105

Engilman, Debra, 95

Espinoza, Dewey, 95–98

Essential questions: defined, 78–79; family studies, 81; health, 81; language arts, 80; science, 80; to shape a school's curriculum, 79–81; social studies, 80–81

Estrogren, 10–11

"Evolution Lab" online simulation, 145–146

Explorers ' Page, 94

"Exploring Prejudice in Young Adult Literature through Drama and Role Play" (teacher-friendly Web site), 118

F

Facial expressions, interpretation of, 7

Family studies, essential questions, 81

Fast-food diets, 154

Fast Food Nation (Schlosser), 154

Female brain: attachment of emotional/sensory detail to events, 8; connection between neurons, 4; and sensory details, 45

Female hormones, 3

Female role models for girls, in literature, 112–113

"Fight or flight" response, 6

Finding the Purpose activity, 57

Finding Your Place in the World activity, 36

Fine Young Man, A (Gurian), 131

Finger spelling, 28

Foreign language assignment, as homework, 143

Frequency Table activity, 32

Frontal lobe: and reading, 110; and social functioning, 62

Future Problem Solving Program International (www.fpsp.org), 91

G

Gender: and nutrition, 153–154; and sleep, 150–151; and stress, 147–148

Gender difference, 14–16

Gender-specific groups, 61–62

Ginott, Haim, 128–129

Girls: blood flow in the brain, 8; dopamine in, 11–12; estrogen levels, 10–11, 22; fight or flight response in, 6; language processing areas, 8–9; left-hemisphere preference, 12–13; and movement while learning, 17–18; and multitasking, 6; and oxytocin, 12; processing of verbal and emotional information, 8; processing/response to classroom information, 4–5; retention in, 7; and sensory processing, 9–10; serotonin levels, 11; spatial processing areas, 9; testosterone levels, 10

Give Water a Hand, 94

Glenbrook Academy of International Studies (Illinois), 83

Gotcha! activity, 27

Graphic Organizer Race, 56

Graphic organizers, 45–48; classifying (activity), 56; on the computer, 52–53; conceptual, 46–47; cyclical, 48; developing, 46; hierarchical, 46; sequential, 47–48; uses of, 46

Great Outdoors: Restoring Student's Right to Play Outside (Rivkin), 23

Greeks (simulation), 102

Group work, 60–61

Group work playbook, 65

Gurian Institute, ix; history of, 2; Training Division, 15

Guys Read (Scieszka), 113

H

Hackett, Buddy, 69

Hamm, Mia, 39–40

Hand fidgets, 26

Health, essential questions for, 81

Healthy choices, 69

Helicopter parents: grounding, 136–138; "How Not to Be a Helicopter Parent," excerpt from, 137

Hierarchical organizers, 46

Hippocampus, 7; and visual-spatial thinking, 45

History assignment, as homework, 143

Homework: assignment suggestions, 145; biology assignment, 143–144; differing boy/girl views of, 144; foreign language assignment, 143; history assignment, 143; math assignment, 143; practical ideas for handling, 146–147; social studies assignment, 143; and teenagers, 142–147; writing assignment, 143

How Can You Move? activity, 29–30

How Many Letters on a Page? activity, 32

How the Brain Learns to Read (Sousa), 110

Human Number Line activity, 31

Humor in the classroom, 90

I

iEarn Projects, 94

iMovie, 53

In a Single Bound: A Short Primer on Comics for Educator (Little), 115

Interactive homework assignments, 144–145

Interviews, as culminating project, 106

Iron, in diet, 153–154

It's Electric! activity, 34

J

Jensen, Eric, 1, 37

Johnson, Carol, 151

Jordan, Michael, 62

K

K-W-L chart, 57

Keel, Yvette, 24

Keller, Helen, 127

Kids Can Make a Difference, 94

Kids Care Project, 94

Koel, Tara, 117

L

Language arts, essential questions for, 80

Language arts activities, 29–30; Back on the Job activity, 30; How Can You Move? activity, 29–30; sentence strings, 30; word charades, 30; word games, 30

Language processing areas, 8–9

Laufer, Rachel, 71

Learning teams, 59–68

Learning to Question, to Wonder, to Learn (McKenzie), 80

Lee, Spike, 109

Left frontal lobe: and choice making, 71; and motivation/engagement, 89

Left-hemisphere preference, 12–13

Lennon, John, 59

Letter writing, as culminating project, 106

Levine, Dr. Mel, 88

Lewis Mills High School (Burlington, Connecticut), use of essential questions by, 81–82

Limbic system, 6–7; and choice making, 71; and motivation/ engagement, 89; and social functioning, 62; and student-teacher bond, 128

Little, Drego, 115

Living on Your Own (class), 98

Lott, Mary, 21

M

Magnetic resonance imaging (MRI), 4

Making contact activity, 27

Male brain: and aggressive/ impulsive responses to anger/ threats, 7–8; and processing of verbal and emotional information, 8; and sensory details, 45

Male-female brain spectrum, 14

Math assignment: as homework, 143; nutritional components for, 154

Math Mania, 30–31

Math Quest (simulation), 101–102

Mathematics activities, 30–32; Are You Right? activity, 31; Frequency Table activity, 32; How Many Letters on a Page? activity, 32; Human Number Line activity, 31; Math Mania, 30–31; Multiples in Motion activity, 31; Olympic Math, 31; Time, Rate, and Distance activity, 32

McKenzie, Jamie, 80, 83

Meet Three People activity, 65–66

Mentors: crucial role of, 127–139; healthy parental involvement, 138–139; "helicopter parents," grounding, 136–138; importance of, 128–129; Intercept Mentor Training Program for teen girls, 129; Interest

Inventory (form), 134; mentoring parents, 133; open the door to parents, 135; practical strategies, 128–138; recruiting, 131; troubled student, reaching out to, 133; what boys need from, 131–132

Mind at a Time, A (Levine), 88

Minds of Boys, The (Gurian/Stevens), 13, 15

Mirror image activity, 27

Mischke, Chris, 21, 100

Misreading Masculinity (Newkirk), 75

Monsters and Myths: Scripts (teacher-friendly Web site), 118

Motor control, 18

Movement: activities for any subject area, 27–29; "anytime" brain breaks, 26–27; and classroom control, 24–25; finding time for, 23–24; language arts activities, 29–30; and learning, 25; mathematics activities, 30–32; music, 35–36; practical ideas for the classroom, 25–26; principal's observations, 24; science activities, 32–35; social studies activities, 35–36; teacher discussions/actions, 20–22; teacher questions and concerns, 21–22

Multimedia tools, 53; presentation tools, 120; student-constructed Web pages, 120; WebQuests, 120–121

Multiples in Motion activity, 31

Multitasking skills, gender differences in, 6

Music, 29, 33, 37; accompaniment, 26, 27; and brain state, 8; and deep breathing activity, 26; and movement, 35–36

Musical chairs, 28

Musical Groups activity, 66

Musical responses to reading, 123

N

National Service-Learning Clearinghouse (NSLC), 94

National Standards for Theater Education (teacher-friendly Web site), 118

Negative stress, 20

Nonverbal signals, interpretation of, 7

Norepinephrine-adrenaline, 44

Nutrition, 152–155; breakfast, importance to learning, 153; and gender, 153–154; poor eating habits, 153; practical ideas regarding, 155

O

Occipital cortex, and reading, 110

Occipital lobes: and social functioning, 62; and visual-spatial thinking, 45

Olympic Math, 31

Orbiting Planets activity, 33

Oxytocin, 12; and motivation/engagement, 89; and social functioning, 62; and stress, 148; and student-teacher bond, 128

P

Paintings, creating on the computer, 53

Palmer, Arnold, 39, 39–40

Parietal lobes: and social functioning, 62; and visual-spatial thinking, 45

Part of a Group activity, 66

Pass It Back strategy game, 22–23

Patton, George S., 37

Pearson, Wendy, 98

Periodic Review activity, 33

Perry, Dr. Bruce, 11

Perseverance, and team building, 63

Photo editing programs, 53

Physical movement, importance in learning, 17–20

Physics Fun activity, 34

Pictographs, 57

Picture-and-symbol exercises, 49–52

Pion, Julianne, 21

Pixels, 53

Plan of action, 39

Playbook: beginning for yourself and each student, 41; creating, 43; development of, 39–40; expanding to include PowerPoint, 53; graphic organizers, 45–46; how it works, 41–42; metaphor of, 43; as models, 40–41; social, 59; teachers in action, 54–56; terminology in, 43; as tool for understanding and directing students, 44; verbal, 44

"Points to Ponder" jar, 19

Positive social development, 59–68

Positron emission tomography (PET), 4

Pound, Ezra, 117
Power of choice, 69–85
PowerPoint, 53
Prefrontal cortex, 6–7
Presentation tools, 120
Processing differences, 8–10; language processing areas, 8–9; sensory system, 9–10; spatial processing areas, 9
Project-based learning, 91–93; student interest survey, 92–93
Public service announcements (PSAs), as culminating project, 106
Published simulation materials, 101–101
Push and Pull activity, 34

R
Reading: artistic and hands-on responses to, 123–124; in the classroom, tips for, 122; as community service project, 125; demonstration responses to, 124; dramatic responses to, 124; and female role models for girls, 112–113; gender preferences in, meeting, 112; integrated, 112–113; integrating multimedia tools and, 119–121; literacy gap, 109–110; musical responses to, 123; National Assessment of Educational Progress report card, 109; reading aloud, 121; reading lists, reconsidering, 111; teacher discussions, 116–117; teaching through comics and graphic novels, 115–116; teachings connecting drama and, 117–119; and technology, 112–113; verbal responses to, 122–123; videography and photography responses to, 125; young adult (YA) literature, teaching with, 114–115
Reading assignment, nutritional components for, 154
Recommended reading, 114–115
Relevance, 87–94; engaging scenarios, 102–105; project-based learning, 91–93; simulation activities, 99–102; social action projects, 93–94; teacher discussions, 95–98

Reticular activating system: and choice making, 71; and motivation/ engagement, 89
Right hemisphere, and visual-spatial thinking, 45
Right-hemisphere preference, 13
Right ventrial striatum, and motivation/engagement, 89
Rivkin, Mary, 23
Roosevelt Middle School, 15–16; improvement at, 16
Rules, and team building, 64

S
Scavenger hunts, 27–28
Schlosser, Eric, 154
School improvement project, as culminating project, 106
Science, essential questions for, 80
Science activities, 32–35; Cell Scrambler, 34; Dramatic Reenactments, 33; It's Electric!, 34; Orbiting Planet, 33; Periodic Review, 33; Physics Fun, 34; Push and Pull, 34; Solids, Liquids, and Gases, 33; Time Marches On, 35; Viruses and Antibodies, 34
Science classroom, and physical models, 54
Scieszka, Jon, 113
Self-Assessment of Learning Style (with Gender Elements Added) (inventory), 96–97
Sensory system, 9–10
Sentence strings, 30
Sequential organizers, 47–48
Serotonin, 11, 44
Set design, 57–58
Shakespearean insults, 98
Simulation activities, 99–102; issue for boys, 100; issue for girls, 99–100; published simulation materials, 101–101; video simulations, 101
Single photon emission computed tomography (SPECT), 4
Skateboard Science (simulation), 102
Sleep: apnea, 151; deprivation, 149–150; and gender, 150–151; practical ideas regarding, 152; school start times, reconsideration of, 151–152

Smart Boys, Bad Grades (Coates/ Draves), 146

Social action projects, 93–94; as culminating project, 107

Social development, and team building, 64

Social functioning, and the brain, 62

Social interactions playbook: adapting, 63–64; ensuring girls have a voice, 64; team building, 63–64

Social playbook, 59

Social relationships, importance to education, 60–63

Social studies, essential questions for, 80–81

Social studies activities, 35–36; Clue Scramble activity, 35; Clue Sort activity, 35–36; Compass Rose Run activity, 35; Dance Through the Ages activity, 36; Dramatic Reenactments activity, 36; Finding Your Place in the World activity, 36; Storytelling activity, 36; Time Travelers activity, 36

Social studies assignment: as homework, 143; nutritional components for, 154

Solids, Liquids, and Gases activity, 33

Sousa, David, 110

Spatial processing areas, 9

Standing up activity, 26–27

Stevens, Kathy, 129

Stock Market Game (SMG) (simulation), 101

Storytelling activity, 36

Strategy domains, v

Stress, 20; in adolescents, 147–149; and gender, 147–148; helping teens deal with, 149; and oxytocin, 148; and testosterone, 148

Stretch! activity, 26

String Geometry activity, 66

Structural differences, 4–8; amygdala, 7; blood flow in the brain, 7; brain stem, 6; cerebellum, 5; cerebral cortex, 4–5; corpus callosum, 6; hippocampus, 7; limbic system, 6–7; prefrontal cortex, 6–7

Structured discussion protocols, 64

Student attire, choice of, 83–84

Student-constructed Web pages, 120

Student Interest Survey, 92–93

Student newspaper, as culminating project, 106

Study agreements, and choice making, 71–72

Super Size Me (movie), 154

Supramarginal gyrus, and visual-spatial thinking, 45

Symbols, 49–52

Synaptic connections, 18

T

Teacher and Child (Ginott), 128–129

Teachers Involve Parents in Schoolwork (TIPS) "Interactive Homework " assignments (John Hopkins University), 144

Team building, 63–64; benefits of, 63–64; Build It, 67; Build It II, 67; characteristics of, 63; Classroom Quilt, 67; Detective, 67; Meet Three People, 65–66; Musical Groups, 66; Part of a Group, 66; and perseverance, 63; and rules, 64; and social development, 64; strategies, 65–67; String Geometry, 66; Teamwork in Action, 67; To Tell the Truth, 66; Telling Yarns, 66; We're Different, We're Alike, 66

Teamwork in Action activity, 67

Technology: document learning through, 106–107; integrating into your classroom, 52–54; and visual-spatial learning, 58

Teenagers: challenge of teaching, 142–143; and homework, 142–147

Tell the Truth activity, 66

Telling Yarns activity, 66

Temporal lobes: and reading, 110; and social functioning, 62

Testosterone, 3, 9, 10; as "chief engineer" of developing male's body/brain, 3; and social functioning, 62; and stress, 148

Thalamus, and visual-spatial thinking, 45

Thoreau, Henry David, 139

Time Marches On activity, 35

Time, Rate, and Distance activity, 32

Time Travelers activity, 36
Toast (editing application), 53
Tolbert, Tony, 54
Trelease, Jim, 121

U
Uniforms, 85
Using Creative Dramatics! (teacher-friendly Web site), 118

V
Vasopressin, and student-teacher bond, 128
Venn diagrams, 46
Verbal responses to reading, 122–123
Video simulations, 101
Videography and photography responses to reading, 124
Vidulich, Ginny, 21, 55, 95
Viruses and Antibodies activity, 34
Visual-spatial learners, and the science classroom, 54
Visual-spatial learning: classifying organizers, 56; classroom rules, 57; comics and graphic novels, 57; drawing to summarize, 57; Finding the Purpose activity, 57; Graphic Organizer Race, 56; pictographs, 57; set design, 57–58; technology, 58; wall displays, 57; word walls, 57

Visual-spatial prewriting, 45
Visual-spatial strategies, 39–58, 55
Vote with Your Feet activity, 29
Vrooman, Marilyn, 15

W
Wahlstrom, Kyla, 151
Walking review, 28
Wall displays, 57
We're Different, We're Alike activity, 66
Web site creation, as culminating projects, 107
WebQuests, 120–121
Wernicke's area, and social functioning, 62
Wheeler, Val, 98
Who's Got Talent? activity, 29
Wilensky, Rona, 90
Wolfe, Patricia, 70
Wonder of Girls, The (Gurian), 13
Word charades, 30
Word games, 30
Word walls, 57
Wright, Jonathan, 116–117
Writing assignment, as homework, 143

Y
Young adult (YA) literature, teaching with, 114–115